POLITICAL THEOLOGY

POLITICAL THEOLOGY

*Contemporary Challenges
and Future Directions*

Michael Welker, Francis Schüssler Fiorenza,
and Klaus Tanner, editors

WESTMINSTER
JOHN KNOX PRESS
LOUISVILLE • KENTUCKY

© 2013 Westminster John Knox Press

Originally published in German by Neukirchener Verlagsgesellschaft: Francis Schüssler Fiorenza, Klaus Tanner, Michael Welker (Hg)., *Politische Theologie*, Theologische Anstöße Bd. 1, Neukirchener Verlagsgesellschaft mbH, Neukirchen-Vluyn. 2011.

First edition
Published by Westminster John Knox Press
Louisville, Kentucky

13 14 15 16 17 18 19 20 21 22—10 9 8 7 6 5 4 3 2 1

Cover design by Lisa Buckley Design
Cover illustration: Ensuper©shutterstock.com
Typesetting by Henning Mützlitz

Library of Congress Cataloging-in-Publication Data
Politische Theologie. English
 Political theology : contemporary challenges and future directions / Michael Welker, Francis Schussler Fiorenza, and Klaus Tanner, editors. — First edition.
   pages cm
 Papers presented at a symposium held on January 8–9, 2010, and sponsored by the Internationales Wissenschaftsforum in Heidelberg.
 ISBN 978-0-664-23951-0 (alk. paper)
 1. Political theology—Congresses. I. Welker, Michael, 1947- editor of compilation. II. Internationales Wissenschaftsforum. III. Title.
 BT83.59.P66513 2013
 261.7—dc23

                                                              2013031709

♾The paper used in this publication meets the minimum requirements
of the American National Standard for Information Sciences—Permanence
of Paper for Printed Library Materials, ANSI Z39.48-1992.

Table of Contents

Introduction

A historical event took place January 8-9, 2010, at the University of Heidelberg in Germany at the Internationales Wissenschaftsforum Heidelberg (IWH).

Heidelberg professors of theology Klaus Tanner and Michael Welker had invited Jürgen Moltmann from Tübingen and Johann Baptist Metz from Münster as well as Elisabeth Schüssler Fiorenza and Francis Schüssler Fiorenza from Harvard for a series of lectures and discussion on Political Theology from Rahner to Ratzinger before a large group of select participants. It quickly became apparent, however, that the scope of the discussions would not be restricted to just one chapter in the recent history of theology in the Roman Catholic Church. During the lectures and animated discussions, a highly nuanced and complex picture of "older" and "newer" Political Theology emerged from the multifaceted interconnections and tensions between political theologies, liberation theologies, feminist theologies, and theologies that see themselves as "postcolonial" or "decolonizing." New, radical variations on the old Political Theology along the lines of Carl Schmitt, especially in the US, were discussed. The goal was an understanding of the future tasks and potential of Political Theology in local and global contexts.

Following this event, all six lectures were revised and expanded for publication. Together with the portraits of the speakers taken by Heidelberg photographer Stefan Kresin, the lectures were published in German and now at last in English as well, which will make them accessible to an even wider audience.

At first glance the essay by Jürgen Moltmann ("Political Theology in Ecumenical Contexts") recalls the beginning of discussions about Political Theology in Germany in the 1960s. Different paths led Moltmann and Metz to develop Political Theology as a socio-critical theology. Despite strong resistance and numerous warnings against the "politicization of the church," they claimed that there is no such thing as an un-political theology, although some theologies may not be conscious of their political dimension. They distinguished their approaches from the old Political Theology of Carl Schmitt, which had sought to shore up the absolute power of the state against the dangers of revolution and anarchy. In contrast to a quasi-religious idealization of the power of the state and the tendency to think in terms of permanent friend-or-foe relationships, the theology they developed was defined by the guiding idea of an eschatological anticipation of the kingdom of God. The reasoning behind this Political Theology was inspired by the vision and practice of ethical and political anticipation of God's future in which human misery and oppression will end and those who have been marginalized and discriminated against will liberate themselves, and their dignity will be respected.

Liberation theology, developed in Latin America in the 1970s (Gustavo Gutiérrez), drew inspiration from Political Theology in an ideologically-divided Europe, while intentionally keeping its distance. Its leading figures, who had been educated in Europe (such as Leonardo Boff and Jon Sobrino), not only became involved in numerous political conflicts in their own societies but also had to contend with attempts to silence them by the hierarchy of the Roman Catholic Church. Feminist theology also gained strength in the 1970s, becoming a global, continually differentiating movement, which has exerted an enormous attraction in many societies and churches.

The growing awareness of the ecological self-endangerment of humanity and conflicts over military armament policies and the superpowers' ideologies of confrontation led in the 1970s and 1980s to the development within Political Theology of a clear profile in the form of theologies of peace and ecological theologies. Around the world many contextual theologies emerged from Political Theology and liberation theology. Moltmann highlights exemplary cases including Black Theology developed most notably in the US, Korean Minjung theology, Japanese Burakumin theology, and Indian Dalit theology. Moltmann identifies the unifying concept in all these forms as a prophetic theology at work even beyond the sphere of the Christian churches.

Johann Baptist Metz ("Two-Fold Political Theology") at first distinguishes his own approach to Political Theology from other political theologies which were developed in reliance on the political metaphysics of the state of Rome and which have continually reemerged in the church in the works of individual church fathers (e.g., Eusebius) as well as in philosophy (e.g., Hobbes), political theory (e.g., Machiavelli), and jurisprudence. In the twentieth century, the Political Theology of Carl Schmitt (1922) belongs to this tradition with its decisionistic concept of the state directed against parliamentary democracy.

Metz sees his own approach as both in continuity and discontinuity with that of his teacher Karl Rahner. Rahner sought a fruitful yet critical engagement between Roman Catholic theology and the spirit of modernity in the form of an "anthropological turn." He combined classical metaphysical theology with a transcendental and mystical theology in a highly effective way.

Metz wants to develop the anthropological turn beyond transcendental and existential intellectual approaches and towards a theology which takes seriously the human being in history and society. He advocates a theology that is "sensitive to time," meaning it has a culture of perception and memory concentrated on those who suffer, the victims of history and society, in light of divine mercy and the divine promise. He postulates Political Theology as a discourse about God which is sensitive to and generates awareness of the suffering of others and proves itself in "seeking justice." The *Deus caritas est* must be augmented by the *Deus et iustitia est*. Metz warns against an abstract Logos theology which seeks, given the hopelessness of time [*Heillosigkeit der Zeit*] (Jacob Taubes), to guide the search for orientation towards a timeless hope [*Zeitlosigkeit des Heils*]. Christian faith as a justice-seeking faith speaks in light of the Passion story of Christ in the name and authority of those who are suffering unjustly and innocently. On this basis together with Rahner he could consider "God as a subject for humanity." On this basis, according to Metz, it is possible to have a universalism of Christian discourse about God that is "capable of pluralism and is non-violent and anti-totalitarian."

In her lecture, Elisabeth Schüssler Fiorenza challenges Political Theology to be more concrete and specific in the form of a critical feminist theology of liberation and a decolonizing Political Theology. She observes astutely that most political theologies, liberation theologies, and postcolonial theologies "lack a critical feminist analysis." The exclusion of women from public cultural and religious consciousness lives on in many forms of progressive and emancipatory theologies. Elisabeth Schüssler Fiorenza identifies "kyriarchal structures" which extend far beyond patriarchal and hierarchical, political, and clerical forms of consciousness and ways of life.

While using seemingly gender-neutral and universalistic modes of thought, Enlightenment modernity conveys and reinforces kyriarchal mentalities. Complex "structures of domination" and oppression "based on race, class, gender, and ethnicity," as well as religious and cultural affiliation and other codes of domination, must be identified and transformed. This is enormously difficult as many diverse forces arise which mutually stabilize and reinforce these systems. Kyriarchal relationships can certainly adopt forms that are partially progressive and emancipatory. They can integrate certain groups and social strata of women while orchestrating conscious or naive cover-ups of the real constellations of power.

By contrast, Elisabeth Schüssler Fiorenza puts forth a paradigmatic and ambitious agenda for a critical and self-critical feminist theology that uncovers the contradictions "between an egalitarian democratic self-understanding and the de facto kyriarchal socioeconomic social structures." She aims for a fruitful synergy between political and feminist theology, and between liberation theology and decolonizing theology, in which the liberation of "women and other people on the margins" becomes the touchstone of the sincerity of all efforts. In the midst of the dominant kyriarchal public spheres (whether visible or latent), she wants to see the establishment of a public sphere of an "ecclesia for women," as a space out of which concrete political, cultural, and religious changes can be conceptualized, and radical democratic and pluralistic relationships can be created.

In his essay "Prospects for Political Theology in the Face of Contemporary Challenges," Francis Schüssler Fiorenza first points out that German Political Theology has developed not only out of the experience of the Nazi dictatorship, but also in response to the growing economism of the postwar period and its ramifications, together with the theologies which accommodated to it. He shows how Latin American liberation theologies distance themselves from these developments and how in the US as well, other underlying circumstances determine direct and indirect approaches to Political Theology.

He sees a two-fold interest in the old Political Theology in the US, which has been reinvigorated. The neoconservative policies of George W. Bush indirectly followed the maxims of Carl Schmitt, a "decisionism" which arrogated to itself absolute, quasi-religious authority: the establishment of rigid friend-or-foe relationships, preemptive warfare, the violation of international conventions, the treatment of prisoners outside the rule of law, the abuse of prisoners of war, the abrogation of human rights—all by appealing to a state of exception, a state of emergency, and the sovereignty of the political leader who decides and proclaims that we are in such a situation.

In response to the Nazi dictatorship, the Universal Declaration of Human Rights (UDHR) adopted by the General Assembly of the United Nations in 1948, the Geneva Convention of 1949, and other international political agreements initiated a major global countermovement against demonic political and military excesses. The limits of these efforts are now apparent in—of all things—an intense international multilateralism with politically-educated elites and constant observation by the media. This state of affairs has led to a renewed and intense interest in Carl Schmitt's work even among intellectuals who see themselves as progressive. Thus, they call into question whether liberal philosophical and political thought is powerful enough to provide adequate direction.

At the center of his critique, Fiorenza sees "democratic paradoxes" in the tensions between the affirmation of the sovereignty of a people and the proclamation of the value of unconditionally renouncing violence; between the affirmation of the cultural identity of particular groups of people and the search for a universal ethos; and between the affirmation of the value of difference and calling for overarching consensus-building, etc. In these tensions Fiorenza sees challenges for a Political Theology of the future.

He first calls for a subtle, multicontextual historical observation which warns against drawing parallels between and trying to schematize related political events such as the French Revolution or the Weimar Period or major epoch-making catastrophes such as the burning of the Reichstag [in 1933] and the destruction of the World Trade Center. He warns against the careless disparagement and relativizing of the regulating dynamics of democracies and human rights conventions, as found in the works of Ratzinger (now Benedict XVI). Using the example of Martin Luther King Jr., he illustrates the persuasive power of religiously-shaped discourse in political contexts—even without the (philosophically-inspired) translation aids called for by Habermas. He notes the growing ability of religious traditions and communities to incorporate the perspectives of other traditions and communities and thus facilitate the preservation of both difference and mutual understanding. He emphasizes religious awareness of and sensitivity to the suffering of victims and the systemic distortions of sin, and a keen awareness not only of the excesses of political chaos, but also of the excesses of authoritarian governmental power. Political Theology thus proves itself to be an immune system which even late modern and partially secularized societies cannot do without.

In his essay ("Political Theology According to Benedict XVI"), Klaus Tanner examines statements relevant to Political Theology in the encyclicals of Benedict XVI. A central phrase in these is "love and truth." The church is a decisive figure for the realization of divine love; it is the "family of God." If politics wishes to be successful in fulfilling its central task of attaining justice, according to Benedict there must be what he calls "an energy input" of the living power of the church, in which the "love kindled by the Spirit of Christ" is at work. This basic conviction is connected to a massive critique of contemporary developments in science, technology, and culture. This conservative cultural critique is especially in line with papal encyclicals before the Second Vatican Council. Although it invokes the "life in Christ" which is normative for "the development of all humanity," what dominates in effect are "speculative and metaphysical forms of argumentation," and abstract reasoning about the relationship between "Reason" [*Vernunft*] or "Intelligence" and "Love" or calls for a "transcendent view of the person."

In keeping with the old Political Theology, the encyclicals invoke a "political world authority" which needs "to be vested . . . with effective power" and "universally recognized" and which is supposed to solve all economic, military, social and ecological problems. This vision is connected to the agenda of a "purification of reason" through the opening of reason "towards transcendence" and to the "supernatural truth of charity." Tanner observes that the Pope attempts to support these statements with an "ontological-metaphysical understanding of natural law" derived from speculation about the Logos in the early church. The young Ratzinger was quite critical of these traditions, and even as a cardinal referred to them with mild skepticism (see below).

Tanner applies these observations critically and self-critically to all forms of Political Theology that do not take seriously social-scientific analysis. He warns against self-congratulations by ecclesial institutions and movements that downplay the relationships and processes of parliamentary democracy. He warns against a critique of liberalism which invokes an ethical consensus without substantiating it with arguments. He appreciates Benedict XVI's attempt to overcome the false oppositions of faith and rationality, and piety and the search for knowledge, by linking reason and love. But he also fears that all approaches seeking to live up to this agenda are nipped in the bud by "ancient unhistorical Logos traditions and ontological natural law doctrines." He recommends paying very close attention to which concepts of the political and the actual political situation are at play when large-scale solutions are being proposed.

Michael Welker ("The Future Tasks of Political Theology: On Religion and Politics since Habermas and Ratzinger") first turns to the meeting between Joseph Ratzinger and Jürgen Habermas in 2004 at the Catholic Academy of Bavaria. The goal of the encounter was to come to an agreement on the "pre-political moral fundamentals of a liberal state." There were high expectations on all sides.

In this discussion Habermas warns against a "derailing secularization," on the one hand, and the view that the liberal secularized state is dependent upon ideological or religious but "at least collectively binding ethical traditions," on the other. He describes the picture of a "democratic process" that is supposedly shaped by "citizens of the state, who see themselves as authors of the law," and "citizens of society, to whom the law is addressed." In this process, systems of religious symbols that have been adequately "translated" could be highly effective at providing a sense of orientation. Most important, however, are a self-critical "policy of remembrance" and a "constitutional patriotism," which upholds the principles of the constitution while evaluating it discursively again and again in new contemporary contexts.

What is helpful for the search for the future tasks of Political Theology is Habermas's insistence on concretely applying all concepts of social transformation concretely through legislation and legal action and the alignment towards the constitution of a state which wishes to be accepted as a "constitutional state" and "welfare state." Yet in contrast to Habermas's early work, the precarious interdependencies in civil societies between communication, politics and law, on the one hand, and the power of the market, media and technology, on the other, are discussed as rarely as in most political theologies. The relevance of the family, the educational system, and the academy for the processes of development and transformation in liberal societies is also not clearly addressed.

While Habermas concentrates on communicative processes in civil society, Ratzinger develops a broad perspective on epoch-spanning and global developments. Yet this breadth does not reflect a corresponding depth and acuity. The uncertainties and weaknesses of Ratzinger's position, which Klaus Tanner's article on Benedict XVI discloses, are based in part on his speculative views derived from natural law, which he wishes to uphold against his better judgment ("this tool has lost its effectiveness, unfortunately"). At the same time, not only are rudimentary approaches from the social sciences lacking, but also any clear and differentiated christological and pneumatological orientation that could counteract the seductive appeal of the old Political Theology with its supposed potential for order.

In contrast, a Political Theology of the future must target three clusters of tasks:

1. It must practice a socio-theoretical prudence that takes into account in a differentiated way a) interpersonal relationships (e.g., "I and the Other," basic friend and family relationships), b) basic and complex social relationships (e.g., initiatives, parishes, political parties, civil societies) and c) relationships that are highly institutionalized in terms of organization and normative claims (e.g., politics, law, science, the market). Those who continually fail to differentiate between the various degrees of cohesion and communication in these contexts, or even superimposes on them d) metaphysical, theistic or mystical forms of thought (e.g., the relationship to God, the connection to the transcendent), will be unable to offer fruitful theological or helpful political guidance. This may be a formidable challenge but one which can certainly be overcome if we consider the example of the young Dietrich Bonhoeffer.

2. A Political Theology of the future requires clearer diagnoses based on social analysis. Most emancipatory theologies still function based on moral appeals within the closed circuit of religion and civil society and hope their message will be amplified by politics, the academy, and the media. There are hardly any usable analyses of the strong influence

which the market, media, technology, and law exert on politics and the communicative processes of civil society—neither general analyses nor those focused on the specific contexts of oppression and impoverishment. The critique of Marx and Engels of the Left Hegelians ("The Holy Family")—who confused loud propagandizing of their political-moral complaints and objectives with the process of bringing about change in social relationships—should give every Political Theology of the future some food for thought. Such a Political Theology can learn to be self-critical in this examination of a socio-critical moralism without thereby being enticed into the trap of an orthodox Marxism. The urgently necessary cooperation between Political Theology and postcolonial theory and the writing of history as well as the development of "decolonizing" theologies (Elisabeth Schüssler Fiorenza) is still in the early stages.

3. A Political Theology of the future must lose its uncertainty about and fear of liberal multicontextual and pluralistic environments. It absolutely must not confuse this inhibition with the fear of obfuscation and the evasive power of evil. It must handle and overcome both insecurities with biblically-shaped pneumatological and christological orientations. A carefully-nuanced theological foundation provides the strength needed for a critical and self-critical engagement with complex social, cultural, religious and ideological problems. Only a nuanced and sophisticated search for justice and truth based on theology and spirituality can, while suffering from unjust relationships and in passionate resistance to oppressive violence, mobilize the prophetic, diaconal, and spiritual powers which can move and transform sociopolitical contexts.

Photo © Stefan Kresin. Used by permission.

Jürgen Moltmann

Political Theology in Ecumenical Contexts

I. The Beginnings of Political Theology in Germany

Johann Baptist Metz came to Political Theology through Karl Rahner. I came to this new frontline of postwar theology in Germany through Karl Barth. Metz took the initiative from within Catholic fundamental theology, while my teaching appointment was for dogmatics and ethics, so that I had to portray the political dimensions in these areas. Auschwitz cast a long shadow over both of us. Our generation had to live in the shadow of the dead from the death camps. At first our Political Theology was a "theology after Auschwitz." Rahner had introduced the "anthropological turn" in modern Catholic theology. Metz went beyond that:

The attempt to read and understand all of theology as anthropology is an important accomplishment of contemporary theological work. Yet this theology "as anthropology" is in danger of losing its sense of history and the world when it is not understand as ultimately eschatology. Only in the eschatological horizon of hope does the world appear as history.[1]

Since he understood my "theology of hope" so well in this point, I gladly took up his offer from my side:

"Every eschatological theology must become a political theology which is a socio-critical theology."[2]

In the theology of Karl Barth and the Confessing Church during the Nazi dictatorship, the importance of the political sermon was discussed, and the "pulpit paragraph" [*Kanzelparagraph*] forbidding church interference in politics, in effect until 1945, was rejected. In

---

[1] Johann Baptist Metz, *Zur Theologie der Welt* (Mainz/München: Matthias-Grünewald-Verlag, 1968), 83. English translation: *Theology of the World* (New York: Seabury Press, 1973).

[2] Ibid., 106. I took this up and pursued it in my own way in "Theologische Kritik der Politischen Religion," in *Kirche im Prozess der Aufklärung*, eds. Johann Baptist Metz, Jürgen Moltmann and Willi Oelmüller (Mainz/München: Kaiser, 1970), 11-51. Further related commentary can be found in this book.

1969 the Cologne "Political Night Prayers" by Dorothee Sölle and Ful-
bert Steffensky took this rejection seriously. Because "Romans 13" had
trained Protestants to obey authorities uncritically, it was only once
chapters 12 and 13 of the Letter to the Romans were interpreted together in a hermeneutically correct fashion that attitudes began to change.
Now theologians were discussing political "worship in everyday life,"
as Ernst Käsemann put it, and Ernst Wolf's new "political doctrine of
virtue," both of which were supposed to replace the metaphysics of the
state. But the resistance to the purported "politicization of the church"
was—and remains—very strong in Protestantism, because Protestantism, in contrast to Roman Catholicism, likes to portray itself as
"underpinning the state." The situation did not change until Political
Theology and the new critical consciousness which it encountered after
1968 took shape.

Political theology was not understood as the theology of the political,
but rather it was a designation for every Christian theology and a her-
meneutical or fundamental-theological category. There is consciously
political theology, there is politically un-conscious theology, but there
is no such thing as an un-political theology, at least not on this earth
and presumably not even in the heavenly *politeuma*.

At that time many books appeared bearing the title of Political
Theology: I can name here only those of Dorothee Sölle, Jan Lochman,
and in El Salvador Ignacio Ellacuria, the late martyr. This shows that
the new Political Theology was ecumenical right away and was
positioning itself within the openness to the future of the Second
Vatican Council with its declarations *Gaudium et Spes* and *Populorum
Progressio*.

The first high point was the Christian-Marxist dialogues of the Paulus-
Gesellschaft in Salzburg, Herrenchiemsee, and Marianske Lasne in the
former Czechoslovakia from 1966 to 1968. Karl Rahner and Roger Ga-
raudy were the speakers, while Ernst Bloch's *Principle of Hope* formed
the background for discussions. Finally, in Marienbad in May 1968
theologians open to the world met Marxists open to God. We were
seeking justice on earth; they were looking for a transcendence which
was not alienating. It was the finest hour in a divided Europe. But at
the end of August in the same year, the lights went out in Europe for 21
years as the Cold War stifled the beginnings of a new Europe.

So "1968" was both the apex and the nadir, the high point and the
crash at the same time[3]: the ecumenical movement reached its peak at
the global conference in Uppsala under the motto "See, I am making
all things new," and the Latin American Bishops' Conference in

---

[3] Jürgen Moltmann, "Siehe, ich mache alles neu: Die ökumenische Bewegung von
Uppsala und Turku 1968 und Bangkok 1972—nicht nur eine Sache der Studenten,"
in *Zwischen Medellin und Paris: 1968 und die Theologie*, eds. K. Füssel and M.
Ramminger (Lucerne/Münster: Exodus Verlag, 2009), 110-124.

Medellin proclaimed the church's "preferential option for the poor." In the U.S. the civil rights movement reached its highest rates of approval, but then on April 4, 1968, Martin Luther King, Jr. was killed. With the Second Vatican Council, the Catholic Church seemed to have better instincts than the Protestant Church in Germany, but the encyclical *Humanae Vitae* was a grievous blow for many Catholic colleagues. In Berlin, Paris, Berkeley, Mexico, and Tokyo, students were protesting against the Vietnam War and calling for a cultural revolution. The new Political Theology was also shaped by these movements and experiences.

II. Carl Schmitt and the Old Political Theology

Unfortunately, the field of Political Theology was already occupied by the old Political Theology of Carl Schmitt, an expert in constitutional law and Nazi state councilor. This led to some confusion until Metz named our concerns the "New Political Theology." Schmitt's Political Theology was the theology of political sovereignty: "Sovereign is the one who decides on the state of exception."[4] Thus, in the 1920s "the dictatorship of the President of the Reich" referred to article 48 of the Weimar imperial constitution. For Schmitt, God and state constitute that sovereignty which should be able to stand up to anarchy as described in Michael Bakunin's *God and the State*. Schmitt did not borrow the term "political theology" from the ancient world but from Bakunin. He saw the conflict between the authority of the state and revolution, or rather anarchy, against the background of the apocalypse of world history. He believed in the idea of the Armageddon, the "last battle," which was the reason in his opinion that the world was already engaged in a permanent civil war here and now. The existential political category is the "friend-or-foe relationship: whoever is not for us, is against us." The archetype for the friend-or-foe relationship is the relationship between God and Satan, which is headed for the decisive battle. Civil liberties are suspended. The dictatorship rules with emergency law in order to fend of impending anarchy. That we have not yet reached this apocalyptical end of history is due to the mysterious *katechon* in 2 Thess 2:7. The power that is delaying the end by restraining evil is, according to Carl Schmitt, the sovereign authority of the state: "I believe in the *katechon*; for me it represents the only possibil-

---

[4] Carl Schmitt, *Politische Theologie: Vier Kapitel zur Lehre von der Souveränität* (1922), 2nd ed. (Berlin: Duncker & Humblot, 1934), 11. English translation of quote by the translator of this article. For more on Schmitt's theology of the political, see Heinrich Meier, *Die Lehre Carl Schmitts: Vier Kapitel zur Unterscheidung Politischer Theologie und politischer Philosophie* (Stuttgart: Metzler, 1994).

ity for understanding and making sense of history as a Christian."[5] For him the campaigns of the Christian emperors against the pagans and infidels, as well as *La Conquista* in Latin America, were the heroic deeds of that divinely-desired *katechon*.

In contrast, the new Political Theology focuses on the Church as subject "with its face towards the world" or to state it more simply: world Christianity. It is not about a metaphysics of the state or an apocalyptic rationale of permanent world war, but rather the political engagement of the church in the world of the poor and Christian commitment to "justice, peace and the integrity of creation."

Instead of the apocalyptic *katechon* which is delaying the future of God, the theme of eschatological anticipation became central in ecumenical ethics after Uppsala 1968:

> We ask you, trusting in God's renewing power, to join in this anticipation of God's kingdom, and already to allow today something to appear of this new creation which Christ will complete on his day.[6]

This was the proclamation made by the Fourth Assembly of the World Council of Church in Uppsala in 1968. Such a consciousness eagerly anticipates the future in which, as Ernst Bloch put it, those who are "weary and heavy-laden" are set free and those who have been "humiliated and insulted" attain their dignity. These forms of ethical and political "anticipation" are theologically justified based on the coming of Christ in this world and his resurrection from the dead. The ethic of the Kingdom of God is the ethic of the Sermon on the Mount, and the ethic of the Sermon on the Mount is a countercultural ethic in a world of injustice and violence.

III. Political Theology and Liberation Theology

After Medellin 1968 a kind of Political Theology emerged in Latin America which Gustavo Gutierrez in 1971 named the "theology of liberation." Before this, some had tried out names like "theology of development" and "theology of revolution" but the name "theology of liberation" struck the right note. In terms of subject matter, Political Theology in a divided Europe and the theology of liberation in poor, oppressed Latin America were one heart and one soul—at least, so I

---

[5] Meier, *Die Lehre Carl Schmitts,* 245. For more on Schmitt's doctrine of the *katechon*, see ibid. 243-252. For more on the *katechon,* see also Dietrich Bonhoeffer, *Ethik,* ed. E. Bethge (München: Kaiser, 1949), 45-46.

[6] *Uppsala spricht: Sektionsberichte der Vierten Vollversammlung des Ökumenischen Rates der Kirchen, Uppsala 1968* (Geneva: WCC, 1968), 1. English translation of this quote comes from Jürgen Moltmann, *A Broad Place: An Autobiography* (Minneapolis: Fortress Press, 2009).

thought until 1975 when a group of students from Argentina and Brazil visited Tübingen and explained to us that they were seeking liberation from the dominance of European culture and theology. They did not read Barth, Bultmann, and Moltmann any more, because Karl Marx had supposedly said that "history is class warfare." When asked where Marx was born, they did not answer. That bothered me, and I wrote an open letter to my friend José Miguez-Bonino in Buenos Aires and criticized the seminary Marxism and juvenile, romantic fascination with revolution.[7] This yielded a lot of criticism. But even Gustavo Gutierrez described Metz and me as "liberal theologians," while calling himself a "liberation theologian," although all the quotations in his first book were European and he only discovered later how "to drink from one's own wellsprings."

For the popes in Rome the red flag was not liberation theology but the Marxism they suspected was behind it. John Paul II had had bad experiences with it in Poland, Benedict XVI in Tübingen. At times, the fear of Marxism took on apocalyptical dimensions. Leonardo Boff had found a fitting formula for the use of Marxism in liberation theology: "Marxist analysis: Yes. Marxist solutions: No."

My problems with the phrase the "preferential option for the poor" are first, that this option is not the option "of the poor," and second, that the poor do not want to be addressed only in terms of that which they lack in relation to the rich, but first in terms of who they are, their strengths, their culture, their race, their gender, their religion, and their ethos.[8]

IV. Developments in Political Theology in Germany

I now conceive of the term Political Theology more broadly than Metz and I did in the beginning as a designation for theological reflection on the concrete political practice of Christianity. *Kairos*, the context, and the community shape the political hermeneutics of the Christian message. I have been personally involved in these developments of concrete political theology, but I was not the initiator.

1. Theology of Peace

A divided Germany was always the center of military confrontations

---

[7] The English version of this letter was published as "An Open Letter to José Míguez Bonino," *Christianity and Crisis* 36 (1976): 57-63.

[8] Moltmann, *Erfahrungen theologischen Denkens: Wege und Formen christlicher Theologie* (Gütersloh: Gütersloher Verlaghaus, 1999), 194-222. English translation: *Experiences in Theology: Ways and Forms of Christian Theology* (Augsburg Fortress Press: Minneapolis, MN, 2000).

between the superpowers. Around 1980 the situation heated up through the mutual arms race. Nowhere in the world were there so many atom bombs warehoused as in West and East Germany. The people responded to this with the peace movement. Human chains stretching from Stuttgart to Ulm and continual protests in Mutlangen indicated protests on a massive scale. The Protestant Church [in Germany] published a position paper on peace; the Reformed Church called out for a *status confessionis*: Either atom bombs or Christ! Historic peace churches such as the Mennonites were the role model for everyone who wanted "to live without armaments." In the demonstrations against nuclear terror, which was called "mutual deterrence"—("The one who shoots first, dies second")—nonviolence was practiced. No violence by demonstrators, no violence against the demonstration! Jesus's Sermon on the Mount became a guideline for many Christians. And because evoking it became "dangerous," West German President Carl Carstens and Chancellor Helmut Schmidt dabbled in political exegesis. The text of the Sermon on the Mount appeared in major daily newspapers. The Federation of Protestant Churches in what was then East Germany solemnly repudiated "the spirit, logic and practice" of weapons of mass destruction.[9] The events of the ecumenical decade of peace were very well attended. From 1980 on every Monday evening a small group met in the *Nikolaikirche* (St. Nicholas Church) in Leipzig to pray for peace. In the fall of 1989 this peace circle served as the initial spark for the massive demonstrations which toppled the East German dictatorship. It was the nonviolent triumph against violence: no violence by demonstrators, no violence against the demonstration! With the cry "We are the people!" Germans struggled for democracy for the first time in their history. It was the first successful revolution in Germany, and a nonviolent one on top of that! That was truly a "miracle." It was "crazy" [*Wahnsinn*], as people in Germany called it at the time.

The consequences for me in terms of how Christians should handle violence were:

 – Do not turn swords into Christian swords, and
 – do not be satisfied with only Christian plowshares,
 – but turn the swords into plowshares.

This is the politics of disarmament while building up a just peace at the same time. This is the conversion of the war industry into a peace industry: turning steel helmets into saucepans. Peace is possible and can be achieved in a violent world through confidence-building measures. For the church of Christ the "long Constantinian era" thus comes to an

---

[9] Moltmann, ed., *Friedenstheologie–Befreiungstheologie: Analysen–Berichte–Meditationen*, KT 26 (München: Kaiser, 1988).

end. The church becomes an ecumenical church of peace independent of the state. The constraints on war through the doctrine of "just war"—according to which essentially there cannot be any war at all—has been turned into something positive through the doctrine of "just peace."

2. Ecological Theology

In 1973 the Club of Rome published its study "The Limits to Growth." The first oil crisis showed the limits of energy resources. Protestant theology quickly exhibited an interest in ecological questions, e.g., Güntner Altner's *Schöpfung am Abgrund: Die Theologie der Umweltfrage* (1974) or Gerhard Liedke's *Im Bauch des Fisches: Ökologische Theologie*.[10]

The German regional churches became aware of their responsibility for the country and created positions for environmental officers. The Green, extraparliamentary opposition group became the political party "Die Grünen". Public consciousness changed quite rapidly from that of a throwaway society to embrace a new ecological awareness. Ecumenical gatherings in Basel and Dresden in 1989 for "Justice, Peace and the Integrity of Creation" generated public awareness of the severe environmental degradation in socialist East Germany. It was already becoming clear at the time that the true horizon of the Christian churches was not the world religions but the cosmos, as was written in the letters to the Ephesians and Colossians.

In my opinion, taking seriously ecological crises, climate change, and growing desertification requires a fundamental systemic change in economy, politics, and lifestyles and consequently a new theological and spiritual paradigm. It began with a reinterpretation of the command to "have dominion" over the earth and leads to overcoming anthropocentric thought in Christian theology. It began with the recognition of God's covenant with the earth and leads to overcoming the exploitation of natural and human resources. Ecological and social injustice and acts of violence are related to each other, thus social and ecological justice must also correspond with each other in order to find a viable peace with nature—if humans are to survive and thrive. Climate change calls for system change! New doctrines of creation have emerged in theology; a "theology of nature" and even a "natural theology" are no longer taboo from a Protestant perspective. Because it is

---

[10] Cf. Güntner Altner, *Schöpfung am Abgrund: Die Theologie der Umweltfrage* (Neukirchen-Vluyn: Neukirchener Verlag, 1974); Gerhard Liedke, *Im Bauch des Fisches: Ökologische Theologie* (Stuttgart: Kreuz Verlag, 1979). For a contemporary discussion, see also Heinrich Bedford-Strohm, ed., *Und Gott sah, dass es gut war: Schöpfung und Endlichkeit im Zeitalter der Klimakatastrophe* (Neukirchen-Vluyn: Neukirchener, 2009).

no longer about recognizing God in nature, but recognizing nature in God.[11]

3. Feminist Theology

Political theology has not spawned a feminist theology, but feminist theology is also a form of political theology. It deals not only with overcoming cultural patriarchalism, but also fighting for "human rights for women."[12] Elisabeth Schüssler Fiorenza, one of the world's leading feminist theologians, is also represented in this volume.

4. Headwind

Political theology originally sought to overcome the privatizing tendencies of personalistic and existentialist theology. But it also reverted after 1980 to the so-called "Me Decade." "Religion" was fashionable again instead of "revolution," whatever "religion" was supposed to mean. Marxist social critique gave way to politically-sponsored "inter-religious dialogue." Whereas Eberhard Jüngel and I had sought to engage in discussions with atheism, the world religions now became the main focus, as though the secular world no longer existed. In many congregations, "third world" groups were replaced with self-awareness encounter groups: Protest was out; meditation was in. Metz and Moltmann disappeared, while Anselm Grün and Jörg Zink kept listeners entertained at the *Kirchentage*.[13] This vogue for self-awareness did not last long, because there were political "signs and wonders": the nonviolent disintegration of the Soviet Empire and the peaceful end of the apartheid regime in South Africa. In Latin America, military dictatorships perished, while in Eastern Europe the "colored" revolutions democratized the socialist dictatorships. Out of a dipolar world a global world came into being with its own new problems.

---

[11] Moltmann, *Gott in der Schöpfung:Ökologische Schöpfungslehre* (München: Kaiser, 1985); Christian Link, *Schöpfung*, vol. I: *Schöpfungstheologie in reformatorischer Tradition*, vol. II: *Schöpfungstheologie angesichts der Herausforderungen des 20. Jahrhunderts* (Gütersloh: Gütersloher Verlagshaus, 1991); Heinrich Bedford-Strohm, *Schöpfung: Ökumenische Studienhefte* 12 (Göttingen: Vandenhoeck & Ruprecht, 2001).

[12] Elisabeth Moltmann-Wendel, *Menschenrechte für die Frau: Christliche Initiativen zur Befreiung der Frau* (München: Kaiser, 1974).

[13] Translator's Note: The Kirchentag is a popular biennial German Protestant Church congress with prominent speakers, panel discussions, musical performances, worship services, and other events.

V. Global Developments in Political Theology

In ecumenical contexts the "theology of liberation" was more influential than political theology, because it provided a concrete catchword instead of addressing just one area for the practice and theology of Christianity.

Below I provide a summary of a loose succession of ecumenically-relevant liberation theologies:[14]

1. *Black Theology* was dedicated to the liberation of African-Americans in the US from white racism. James Cone from Union Theological Seminary wrote a "Black Theology" in 1971, which sought to unite protesting Christians with the Black Power movement. We immediately incorporated the translation provided by Frederick Herzog into our series *Politische Theologie*,[15] but found little understanding in Germany. In the American protests against white racism and the sociocultural repression of the descendants of the black slaves, black theology became controversial and very influential—if my assessment is accurate—especially among white Christians and theologians. The black protest movement had two leaders: the nonviolent Martin Luther King, Jr. and Malcolm X, who was prepared to use violence. Throughout his life Jim Cone attempted to connect both of them.[16]

2. *Minjung Theology* was developed in South Korea by the New Testament scholar Byung Mu Ahn.[17] Ahn had studied in Heidelberg and wrote his dissertation about Jesus and the *ochlos* in the Gospel of Mark. After returning to Korea to the Hankuk Seminary, he translated *ochlos* into *minjung* and with his Galilee congregation in Seoul he sup-

---

[14] For a more detailed treatment of this topic, see Moltmann, *Erfahrungen theologischen Denkens: Wege und Formen christlicher Theologie,* Chapt. III: "Spiegelbilder befreiender Theologie: Schwarze Theologie für Weiße"; "Lateinamerikanische Befreiungstheologie für die Erste Welt"; "Minjung-Theologie für die herrschenden Klassen"; "Feministische Theologie für Männer"; "Unbeantwortete Fragen," (Gütersloh: Gütersloher Verlagshaus, 1999), 166-265. English translation: *Experiences in Theology: Ways and Forms of Christian Theology* (Augsburg Fortress Press: Minneapolis, MN, 2000).

[15] James H. Cone, *Black Theology and Black Power* (New York: Harper & Row, 1969); G. S. Wilmore and J. H. Cone, *Black Theology: A Documentary History 1966-1979* (Maryknoll, New York: Orbis Books, 1979).

[16] Cone, *Martin & Malcolm & America: A Dream or a Nightmare?* (Maryknoll, NY: Orbis Books, 1991).

[17] Byung-Mu Ahn, "Draußen vor der Tür: Kirche und Minjung in Korea, Theologische Beiträge und Reflexionen," in *Theologie der Ökumene,* vol. 20, ed. Hans-Werner Gensichen and Theo Sundermeier (Göttingen: Vandenhoeck & Ruprecht, 1986); Wolfgang Kröger, *Die Befreiung des Minjung: Das Profil einer protestantischen Befreiungstheologie für Asien in ökumenischer Perspektive* (München: Ch. Kaiser, 1992); Moltmann, ed., *Minjung: Theologie des Volkes Gottes in Südkorea* (Neukirchen-Vlyun: Neukirchener Verlag, 1984).

ported projects by working people. Like the Korean Minjung, he was persecuted by the military dictatorship and sentenced to time in prison. I know him well along with the cofounder of this movement, Nam Dong Suh. I was fascinated by how an exegetical discovery—the active role of the *ochlos* in the history of Jesus according to Mark—had generated a contemporary Christian movement for liberation. This has not happened often since Luther's discovery of justification Gospel. Today there are many Minjung pastors in Korea, although Minjung theology has lost some ground. Why? As my friend David once stated ironically: "Ever since Minjung in Seoul drive cars . . .," they are no longer the oppressed poor.

3. In considering local, contextual liberation theologies, I would like to mention two here: *Burakumin theology* in Japan and *Dalit theology* in India. They both deal with the freedom of those in particular societies who have been excluded and oppressed. The Burakumin in Japan are the "unclean" workers, who have been excluded from Japanese society for centuries. Their liberation movement originated at the beginning of 1920 and still uses the thorn of crowns as their symbol today, though without the crucified Nazarene. In the middle of the 1990s, Christian theology developed a liberation theology of the Burakumin. In India the casteless Dalit have been excluded for thousands of years for racist, cultural, and religious reasons and have been condemned to poverty and unclean work. Dalit theology attempts to break through the fatalistic belief in Karma and to move the Dalit to embrace their human dignity and revolt.

Two problems result when liberation theology is expanded and transferred to other contexts:

1.   In Latin America, the poor are consistently Christians. Christian theology brings them liberation and justice in the name of Jesus Christ. In Asia, however, the majority of the poor and oppressed —except in Korea and the Philippines—are Shintos or Hindus or Muslims. They require freedom from their oppression but not Christian theology.
2.   For this reason, in these areas the Christian motives for action are weaker and the humanist or Marxist motives stronger. The poor should move from being passive objects in the history of the powerful to becoming active subjects in their own personal histories. When they rise up from subjugation to freedom, they become the vanguard of a liberated humanity. This arising to become a subject and embrace equality does not require Christian theology, except where the goal is to initiate Christians into this project of humanity so that they might participate in it.

So what do Political Theology in Europe and liberation theology in the developing nations have in common?

The famous Kairos Document, which contributed to the overthrow of the inhuman apartheid regime in South Africa, distinguished between: 1. Church theology, 2. State theology, and 3. Prophetic theology.

Political Theology as prophetic theology *is* liberation theology, and liberation theology is Political Theology.

Photo © Stefan Kresin. Used by permission.

Johann Baptist Metz

Two-Fold Political Theology

I.

Let us begin with a (too?) simple distinction: the distinction between
the old, to a certain extent "classical," political theology and the new
political theology. We will review the first with just a brief historical
perspective. This "classical" political theology predominantly understands the term "political" in terms of national and legal policy. This
use is certainly supported by the basic intention of the traditional term
"political theology." Ultimately, discourse about "political theology"
goes back to the Stoics and their three-part distinction between mythical, natural, and political theology. Thus this political theology in ancient Rome served the religious legitimization of the "absolute" and
"infallible" state. This Roman political metaphysics of the state is reflected in early Christian theologies, for example, in the so-called
Byzantine *Reichstheologie* of Eusebius. Above all, Roman political
theology was taken up again in the Renaissance—first by Machiavelli,
then Hobbes. Finally, it influenced the Enlightenment and positions
critical of democracy in French Traditionalism while also impacting
the restorative idea of a "Christian state" in political Romanticism and
Right Hegelian theories of law and the state. Under the influence of
these traditions Carl Schmitt in the last century could propound his
Political Theology (first published in 1922) and justify his general opposition to the Weimar Republic and parliamentary democracy in favor
of a strict, decisionistic idea of the state instead. I cannot discuss in de-
tail here the relationship between the political theology of Schmitt and
the thought of Leo Strauss and his recourse to the classical concept of
natural law, as well as the more recent history of the reception of
Schmitt's ideas in Europe and the USA.[1]
Although this political theology of the state has continued to receive attention again and again—especially in times of intensified instability—
Carl Schmitt himself spoke the closing word (1963) for this political
theology: "The era of statism [*Staatlichkeit*] is now coming to an end.

---

[1] Cf. the references in Jürgen Manemann, *Carl Schmitt und die Politische
Theologie: Politischer Anti-Monotheismus* (Münster: Aschendorff Verlag, 2002),
esp. 201-213.

We should not waste another breath discussing it."[2] It would have been
nice if the Society of Saint Pius X (SSPX) and other sympathizers in
the Vatican had also known this! Yet they continue, undiminished, to
do political theology as an ideology of statism—in search of the
"Catholic state."

II.

Let us now turn our attention to the new political theology. I am referring especially to the situation in Catholic theology, always with ecumenical intentions, of course (which my friend Jürgen Moltmann will
no doubt confirm). To keep this within the desired length, I will depict
the beginning of this new political theology from the perspective of my
own theological biography.[3] It has been shaped in particular by one
name, that of my teacher and my friend Karl Rahner. Through him I
worked my way into the discourse of the Catholic theological tradition.
With his "anthropological turn" of the discourse of God, Rahner
guided Catholic theology into a productive but critical engagement
with the spirit of modernity as hardly anyone had done before him. My
critical issues with Rahner relate to how this "anthropological turn" is
carried out. In my opinion, it cannot be purely undertaken according to
a philosophy of consciousness—that is, not in line with the concept of
transcendental identity—but rather, from the start we must keep in
mind humankind in history and society, that is, the anthropological turn
must proceed in line with a dialectical concept of temporality. Perhaps
I should have always labeled this concern as a form of "dialectical
theology" (whereby "dialectics" stands in particular for the critique of
the timelessness and lack of a sense of history in the Logos of Christian
theology). Instead I referred only to "political theology"—and was
probably too insouciant about the semantic pressure which "classical"
political theology (from the Stoics to Carl Schmitt) would exercise on
this terminology.[4] The new political theology uses this term in any case

---

[2] Quoted here according to Robert Spaemann, "Legitimer Wandel der Lehre,"
Frankfurter Allgemeine Zeitung (October 1, 2009), 7.

[3] Cf. especially Metz, *Zur Theologie der Welt* (Mainz: Matthias-Grünewald-Verlag,
1968); *Glaube in Geschichte und Gesellschaft: Studien zu einer praktischen
Fundamentaltheologie*, 5th ed. (Mainz: Matthias-Grünewald-Verlag, 1992) with a
new preface; *Zum Begriff der Neuen Politischen Theologie 1967-1997* (Mainz:
Matthias-Grünewald-Verlag, 1997); *Memoria Passionis: Ein provozierendes Gedächtnis in pluralistischer Gesellschaft* (Freiburg: Herder, 2006). Cf. also "Geschichte wagen: Ein Brief über Treue zu Karl Rahner," in *Gotteswege: Für Herbert
Vorgrimler*, ed. Ralf Miggelbrink, Dorothea Sattler and Erich Zenger (Paderborn:
Schöningh, 2009), 63-67. For more on this "outlook on history" in the "Paradigm of a
New Political Theology," see especially J. Reikerstorfer, *Weltfähiger Glaube: Theolo-
gisch-politische Schriften* (Münster: Lit Verlag, 2008).

[4] For new, quite pointedly critical remarks on the issues of the new political theo-

with a strictly theological intention. It called itself "political" first of all as an identification of its correctivist objection to a post-Scholastic Catholic theology, which attempted, with its tendency towards an undialectical privatization of its Logos (which has since been interpreted anthropologically), to go beyond the challenges of the political Enlightenment without having properly engaged it.

From the beginning, this new political theology was about a theological reevaluation of the processes of modernity which had already begun in late Scholasticism and above all in nominalism, and especially the processes of political Enlightenment with the associated turn towards "the political," without thereby engaging in an undialectical adaptation blind to the inner contradictions of these modern learning processes.

In his most recent interview with Eduardo Mendieta, Jürgen Habermas confirms that there are also two kinds of political theology for him: one which is anti-Enlightenment and—in view of the new political theology—one which adopts the traditions of the Enlightenment and which, given its "sensitivity to time," is able to build a bridge between philosophy and contemporary theology.[5] My critical reservations about Habermas relate to his undialectical characterization of the idea of "temporality" with the word "post," whereby we live in a post-traditional, in a post-metaphysical ... time, as if "tradition" and "metaphysics," etc. had no active and operative presence anyway, not even in the sense of a negative dialectic of the knowledge of the absent. With this critical remark, the new political theology (which—I realize I am repeating myself—can indeed be understood as a new form of "dialectical" theology) is not calling into question its affirmation of the learning processes of modern reason and the resulting political Enlightenment, but rather only calling attention to this: When modern Reason in the name of enlightenment seeks to withdraw completely and utterly from the historical dialectic of remembering and forgetting, where it then abandons the "dialectic of the Enlightenment" in favor of a rationality which is free of remembering and narrating and in this sense purely discursive, then, in my opinion, it inevitably bases the modern processes of Enlightenment on forgetting and thus stabilizes the prevailing cultural amnesia with its extremely weak awareness of that "which is

---

logy, see both the *Jahrbuch Politische Theologie,* vol. 5 (2008), edited by Jürgen Manemann and Bernd Wacker and published under the title *Politische Theologie – Gegengelesen* (Münster: Lit Verlag, 2008). Cf. my essay "Mit dem Gesicht zur Welt: Eine theologisch-biographische Auskunft," 1-9) as well as *Theologisch-politische Vergewisserungen,* ed. Thomas Polednitschek, Michael J. Rainer and José A. Zamora (Münster: Lit Verlag, 2009). Finally, many passages in the book *Mehr als das Ganze: Nachdenken über Gott an den Grenzen der Moderne* (Ostfildern: Matthias-Grünewald-Verlag, 2008) by Tiemo R. Peters can be read as a productive, critical treatment of the issues of the new political theology.
[5] *Deutsche Zeitschrift für Philosophie* 58 (2010), 3-16, here: 16.

absent," which "cries out to heaven." Strengthening and keeping this consciousness alive in the public sphere belongs to "the political" in the present era of its social existence, and thus to the "concept of the political" in the New Political Theology, which knows very well how to distinguish between the secularization of the state and the dialectic of secularization in society.[6] For this reason it also regards the "bourgeois religion" that arose in the process of the undialectical adaptation to the societal processes of Enlightenment as anything but a convincing reiteration of the foundation story of Christianity in European modernity.[7]

III.

The New Political Theology understands itself as a fundamental theology. It wishes to elucidate the Christian discourse about God in this time. It wishes to be a discourse about God that is sensitive to temporality and in this sense also committed to learning. How do we talk about God today?[8]

I will take Rahner as my starting point once again. He was always a theological universalist. He fought back against the ecclesiological encryption of discourse about God. For him the God of the Biblical and Christian traditions was not a topic for the church alone, but for all humanity. Was that perhaps already "his" political theology after all? As always, in keeping with Rahner's anthropological mode in the discourse about God, the New Political Theology sought a publicly-accessible understanding for an antitotalitarian, strictly nonviolent universalism of Christian discourse of God which was amenable to pluralism. Also for today. Especially for today. But Christian discourse about God can only be universal in the sense of a "concrete universalism" when it proves itself to be, at its core, sensitive to the suffering of

---

[6] The well-known axiom by Böckenförde that "the liberal secular state lives on premises it cannot itself guarantee" does not refer directly to religion, but rather society. Admittedly, even Jürgen Habermas emphasizes in an interview in 2010 that "[t]he concept of the political which has been transferred from the state to civil society retains a relationship to religion, even within the secular constitutional state." Quoted in German in Jürgen Habermas and Eduardo Mendieta, "Ein neues Interesse der Philosophie an der Religion? Zur philosophischen Bewandtnis von postsäkularem Bewusstsein und multikultureller Weltgesellschaft," *Deutsche Zeitschrift für Philosophie* 58: 1 (2010), 3-16.

[7] Cf. Metz, *Jenseits bürgerlicher Religion: Reden über die Zukunft des Christentums* (Mainz: Matthias-Grünewald-Verlag 1980).

[8] "Gott ist 'immer' gerade 'heute' Gott." [God is 'always' God to us 'today'.] For more on this proposition by Dietrich Bonhoeffer, cf. the interpretation by Tiemo R. Peters, *Mehr als das Ganze: Nachdenken über Gott an den Grenzen der Moderne*, p. 11ff.

others and committed to seeking justice through sympathy and action.[9] *Deus caritas est*: God is Love. This was the emphasis of the first major encyclical of Benedict XVI. Certainly this is true, yet there is a second biblical name for God which also resonates and is affirmed in the New Testament's message and which thus Christians ought not to forget: *Deus et iustitia est:* God is also justice. For the Christian faith, justice is not only a political or only a social-ethical subject, but a strictly theological one: a reasonable confession about God and his Christ. Justice as God's name may seem unimportant for discourse about a Platonic God of Ideas, but it is indispensable for the God of History to which the Bible witnesses. This name for God always exposes the biblically-based discourse of God to the historical experience of human beings anew. Thus this discourse about God must be sensitive to temporality, which not only explains but also experiences, not only teaches but also learns. For at the root of this Biblical name of God, a pending question of justice always lies dormant: the question of justice for the innocent and unjustly suffering victims of our historical existence.

The literary context for the relationship between the question of God and the question of justice can be discovered in the biblical texts and their theodicy—that is, the passion story of humanity is inserted from the very beginning into the message of the salvation of humanity which creates justice. The language of these traditions seeks to recall the cries of the human being and to give the world its temporality, that is, its time limit. The late incursion of the concept of time and temporality into the religions and cultures of the world through biblical apocalypticism—supported by the prophets' language of crisis and the language of suffering in the psalms—is now widely accepted in the study of religious and cultural history. This "temporalization of the world," this turn of "eternal time" into its "temporalization"—that is, into its time limitation—may well be considered a unique characteristic of Judeo-Christian religion within the religious history of humankind. The biblical concept of time was unknown not only in the Near East but also in Greek and Mediterranean religious and cultural spheres, and this applies both to the idea of "eternal time" of the Pre-Socratics (a quasi-postmodern idea revived by Nietzsche also) and to the idea of the "eternal cosmos" in Greek classical thought. So it should come as no surprise that not only the early Christian Platonists, but also Christian Aristotelian such as Thomas Aquinas were at great pains defending the

---

[9] This "concrete universalism" is aware of its underpinnings by the negative dialectics of the *memoria passionis*, the remembrance of extrinsic suffering. Here we see the influence of the works of Walter Benjamin and especially Theodor W. Adorno and from both of their "negative metaphysics." For more on this from New Political Theology circles, see the excellent work on Adorno by José Zamora, *Krise – Kritik – Erinnerung: Ein politisch-theologischer Versuch über das Denken Adornos im Horizont der Krise der Moderne* (Münster: LIT Verlag, 1995).

temporalization of the world (in the doctrines of creation and eschatology). Where they were not successful, there was always the threat that the biblical message about time would be undermined and turn into a dualistic Gnosis with its axiom of the hopelessness of time and the timelessness of hope (Jacob Taubes)—a danger which has dogged the Logos of Christian eschatology almost from its inception (since Marcion).

At their core the apocalyptical texts of the Bible are absolutely not foolish fantasies of doom, perhaps radicalized by zealots, but literary witnesses to a perception of the world that seeks to "reveal" the faces of the victims, witnesses of a worldview that "exposes" what is "really the case" (cf. Rev. 1:9)—counter to the recurring tendency in all other worldviews towards mythical or metaphysical concealment of the horrible calamities in the world and counter to every form of cultural amnesia, which today also makes those who have suffered in the past invisible and their cries inaudible.

Biblical apocalypticism "exposes" signs of the suffering in the history of humanity. It can be a motivation to formulate each major narrative, each "metanarrative" which—after the Enlightenment critique of religion and ideology, after Marxism and Nietzsche and the postmodern fragmentation of history—still remains for us today as the ability to read the world as a Passion story of humanity.[10] "Blessed are those who mourn," Jesus says in the Sermon on the Mount. "Blessed are the forgetful," Friedrich Nietzsche announces as prophet of postmodernity. But what would happen if someday people could only defend themselves against the calamities and suffering in the world with the weapon of forgetting? If they could only build their own happiness based on the victim's merciless forgetting, that is, on a cultural amnesia in which a supposedly endless time is supposed to heal all wounds? Where could resistance for the sake of those who are innocent and suffer unjustly in the world still draw strength? What would then provide inspiration to seek a greater justice and fight for a level playing field of equality for humanity in the One World? And what would happen if in our secular world the vision of ultimate justice in the end was permanently extinguished?

Among the present array of "spiritualities," Christians must be reminded of the basic messianic character of Christianity and its spirituality. Jesus's perspective is first and foremost a messianic one. It does not see first the sin of the other, but his or her suffering.[11] This

---

[10] In my opinion, those forms of universality that make discourse about the biblical God into a nonviolent discourse capable of pluralism can thus be expressed in such a way—*via negativa*, in a kind of negative dialectics of the remembrance of suffering—that they become a topic for the church and for all humanity.

[11] The emphasis on this messianic perspective of the New Testament message seeks above all to be a corrective (as with so much that I do), a corrective of the danger of a one-sided absolutism of sin, which continually resurfaces in the history

messianic sensitivity to suffering has nothing to do with self-pity or a mirthless cult of suffering. It has everything to do, however, with a biblical mysticism of justice: God's passion as an active compassion, a practical mysticism of compassion. A Christianity that prioritizes its biblical roots will continually be faced with this.

Have Christians perhaps bowed out much too quickly and much too early from the genuinely Biblical question of justice? Has Christianity interpreted itself—over the course of time—too exclusively as a religion sensitive to sin and too little to suffering? Why, for example, does the church always have a much harder time with innocent victims than with guilty perpetrators? Such a question cannot be settled in a purely speculative way, and certainly not with purely moral appeals. But perhaps it can with an ecclesiastical understanding of law which first emphasizes the saving justice for the innocently-suffering victims and the perpetrators who suffer from their guilt. Pursuing and addressing this question more precisely has been a problem until today for the New Political Theology. It has asked too little about the relationship between justice and law, between the eschatological justice of God and canonical law.

In any case, Christian faith is a faith that seeks justice. Certainly, Christians are also always mystics at the same time, but never exclusively mystics in the sense of spiritual self-experience, but in the sense of a spiritual experience of solidarity. Above all they are "mystics with open eyes." Their mysticism is not a faceless nature mysticism. Rather, it moves towards an encounter with the suffering other, towards the face of the unfortunate and the victim. It obeys the authority of those who suffer. This obedience leads to an experience which, while it is not a secular equivalent to this mysticism of justice, may foreshadow the earthly appearance of God's proximity in his Christ: "Lord, when did we ever see you suffer? ... And he answered them: Truly, truly, I say to you, whatever you did to the least of these, you have done to me." (Matthew 25).

With this impulse from biblical apocalypticism and its pathos for justice, the Logos of the New Political Theology which is sensitive to time and suffering also becomes involved in the fight for a universal authority in a strictly pluralistic world community. What is to keep our globalized world from imploding after all in uncontrollable religious and cultural battles, for example, here Christianity, there Islam, here the West, there the Middle East? What is it that can hold our world together in peace during this time of globalization? The proposition of the elementary equality of all people, this strongest assumption about humanity, has a biblical foundation. Its moral expression, in which it is accepted from Christianity and proclaimed with the message of the indivisible unity of love for God and love for the neighbor, of God's pas-

---

of the church.

sion and active compassion, goes as follows: There is no suffering in the world that does not concern us. Thus this statement of the elementary equality of all people refers to the recognition of an authority which is available and acceptable to all people, to the authority of those that suffer, of those who suffer innocently and unjustly. It appeals to an authority that is binding for all people before every agreement and rapprochement, indeed everyone, whether religious or secular, and thus cannot be undercut and relativized by any human culture demanding the equality of all people and certainly no religion, not even by the church. For this reason also, recognition of this transcultural authority would be such a criterion which could provide orientation for religious and cultural discourse in a globalized context. It would ultimately be the basis for an ethic of freedom for a strictly pluralistic global public.

Photo © Stefan Kresin. Used by permission.

Elisabeth Schüssler Fiorenza

Critical Feminist The*logy of Liberation
A Decolonizing Political The*logy

Since there are many different forms of feminist the*logy,[1] it is important to emphasize that I am not speaking here as the representative of feminist the*logy[2] as a whole, but am only representing my own theoretical approach of a critical feminist the*logy that understands itself as a decolonizing political the*logy of liberation. Although I understand my approach as explicitly political and decolonizing and in line with the tradition of liberation the*logy, I hesitate to label a critical feminist the*logy simply as liberation the*logy, postcolonial the*logy,[3] or political the*logy. This is the case because all three forms of progressive the*logy have not theorized the fact that until quite recently all wo/men[4] without exception were excluded from the*logy and the

---

[1] On the development of feminist the*logy in Germany, cf. Gisela Matthiae, Renate Jost, Claudia Janssen, Annette Mehlhorn and Antje Röckemann, ed., *Feministische Theologie: Initiativen, Kirchen, Universitäten – Eine Erfolgsgeschichte* (Gütersloh: Gütersloher Verlaghaus, 2008). For a theoretical account, cf. Regina Ammicht Quinn, "Re-Vision von Wissenschaft und Glaube: Zur Geschlechterdifferenz in der Theologie," in *Genus: Geschlecherforschung/ Gender Studies in den Kultur- und Sozialwissenschaften,* ed. Hadumond Bussmann and Renate Hof (Stuttgart: Alfred Kröner Verlag, 2005), 559-589.

[2] The*logy comes from the Greek *theo/a legein* = to speak about G*d. As G*d is neither feminine nor masculine, it is not enough, as Carol Christ has suggested, to replace the masculine spelling *theo* with the feminine *thea*. In order to identify how our speaking about G*d in gendered terms falls short, in my books *Discipleship of Equals* and *But She Said,* I adopted the Orthodox Jewish representation of the name of G-d, which indicates that the name G*d is unspeakable. However, some Jewish feminists pointed out to me that such a spelling affected them negatively, because it suggests a very conservative, or even reactionary, theological frame of reference. For this reason I started to write the word G*d in this form in order to raise awareness through a visual cue that our thought and speech about the divine are androcentric and to destabilize such masculine connotations.

[3] I do not understand my own work as postcolonial the*logy, because postcolonial theories frequently lack a critical feminist analysis. Rather, I understand it as a critical feminist the*logy, whose processes of consciousness-raising (or conscientization) have the effect of being decolonizing. See my book, *The Power of the Word: Scripture and the Rhetoric of Empire* (Minneapolis: Fortress Press, 2007), 111-129.

[4] Postmodern feminist studies have problematized the essentializing function of the categories "woman/feminine." Critical postcolonial and liberation studies have

academy and, in many countries, still are. The largest portion of the poor and disenfranchised were—and still are—wo/men and their children, who in the three forms of progressive the*logy named above, are not taken into account.

I. A Critical Feminist Political The*logy of Decolonizing Liberation

The religious and cultural exclusion of wo/men from public and academic awareness occurs first and foremost through language.[5] Feminist theory and the*logy have again and again pointed out that androcentric or, better put, kyriocentric language, functions as language of domination because it marginalizes or even makes unseen the presence of wo/men in society and church as well as makes our historical actions invisible. It excludes wo/men as acting subjects from public discourse and consciousness by subsuming wo/men under the supposedly generic masculine and by trivializing our adamant demand for recognition.

This exclusion of wo/men from public cultural and religious consciousness does not take place through language alone, however. Wo/men were not only excluded by law and custom from the*logy and academy for centuries, but were also forbidden to speak with authority in the public spheres of church and society. I remind you of just a few scriptural texts, such as 1 Cor. 14 ("Women should be silent in the churches") and 1 Timothy, which forbids a woman to teach and exercise authority over men, or the contemporary papal ban against arguing in public for wo/men's ordination or the ethics of abortion.

A critical feminist the*logy of decolonizing liberation is thus firstly a "dangerous memory" of the many wo/men who have acted and spoken in the name of G*d and continue to do so, yet whose actions in society, church, and the*logy have often been—and still are—passed over with

---

warned against abstracting the feminist- theoretical analysis of gender from its sociopolitical function, because in so doing they reinforce the cultural ideal of the white "lady." This problematizing of the basic categories of feminist analysis has led to a crisis in the self-understandings and practices of the feminist subject. I tried to mark this crisis by writing "wo/men" in a fractured form. This spelling attempts not only to problematize the category of "woman," but also to show that "women" are not a homogenous social group, but are fragmented through structures of race, class, ethnicity, religion, heterosexuality, colonialism, and age. I introduced this form of writing because I do not believe feminists can completely give up the social-collective term "wo/men" and replace it with the analytical category of "gender," unless we wish to marginalize or obliterate the presence of wo/-men in and through our own feminist discourses. (Since this spelling is not possible in German, in German I write *Frauen* in italics and add "and other *Untermenschen*" to elucidate my meaning.)

[5] Hadumod Bussmann, "Haben Sprachen ein Geschlecht? Genus/Gender in der Sprachwissenschaft," in *Genus: Geschlecherforschung/Gender Studies in den Kultur- und Sozialwissenschaften*, 483-518.

silence or responded to with persecution. One might recall here the bloody history of the witch-hunt or the Beguines, who were part of a religious renewal movement towards the end of the Middle Ages and were accused and banned because they were living freely and according to their own will and desires.

Since, *all* wo/men—*whether white, black, African, Asian or indigenous* —were and still are excluded from the*logical teaching authority and since the*logy served as the paradigm for all other academic disciplines until the modern era, the academic disciplines have followed the model of academic the*logy and constituted themselves as male academic disciplines that exclude wo/men. However, we must not forget that, just as all other academic disciplines, so also the*logy has been made possible even until today by the work of wo/men and other subordinated working people.

As long as this explicit exclusion of wo/men from the public sphere of the*logy, church, and academy is not examined critically and acknowledged publicly, academic the*logy, just as all the other academic disciplines, will continue to be forced either to legitimate the marginalization and exclusion of wo/men with theoretical the*logical arguments or to ignore it with silence. Neither the new political the*logy nor liberation and postcolonial the*logies, which are also male dominated, have examined the*logically the exclusion and exploitation of wo/men nor have they made it a central point of their analysis.

Thus, it is not surprising that in establishment-scholarship the prejudice against feminist theory and the*logy lingers on in the form of accusing it of ideology. Feminist research, it has been claimed time and again, is ideological. It allegedly uses academic research methods solely to corroborate preconceived outcomes. From the perspective of feminist scholarship, on the other hand, such an accusation seeks, whether consciously or not, *to hide the dominant scholarship's own ideological beholdenness and its own marginalizing interests.*

Hence, I prefer an understanding of "feminist" which may appear at first glance very simplistic and modern, but which after careful reflection reveals itself to be a complex, postmodern challenge to modernity. A popular bumper sticker in the North American wo/men's movement defines feminism as "the radical notion that women are people." Feminism is the radical conviction that wo/men are full citizens with all rights and duties. This means, according to Habermas, "free and equal individuals who regulate their life together themselves in the course of democratic will-formation."[6]

---

[6] Jürgen Habermas, "Die neue Intimität zwischen Politik und Kultur," in *Die Zukunft der Aufklärung,* ed. Jörn Rüsen, Eberhard Lämmert, and Peter Glotz (Frankfurt: Suhrkamp, 1988), 65.

In brief: I understand the term "feminist" to denote a theory and practice concerned with abolishing systems of domination and with creating radical democratic conditions and attitudes. This approach thus takes up the democratic claim of modernity, while at the same time making it clear, in keeping with postmodernism, that the European Enlightenment has not upheld its claim to universality from its very beginning. The theoretical and practical contradiction between a kyriarchal and an egalitarian society and ethos thus continually produces discursive systems of legitimation that seek to "normalize" and naturalize kyriarchal relations.

According to this understanding, feminist the*logy is a critical, political the*logy of decolonizing liberation which is committed to the societal and ecclesial struggles for the emancipation of wo/men and other people at the margins. In contrast to male-defined liberation and postcolonial the*logies, feminist the*logy does not simply adopt a Marxist or postcolonial cultural analysis. Unlike some research on the feminine or gender, it also does not simply adopt the dualistic theoretical framework of a functionalist gender analytics. Instead, it shifts its emphasis to a complex radical democratic societal analysis of "kyriarchally" interwoven and mutually multiplicative structures of domination. What do I mean with the term *kyriarchal*?

II. Political[7] The*logy: Kyriarchy[8] and Democracy

Kyriarchy is a neologism which I coined; it is derived from the Greek *kyrios* = slave-master or lord and *archein* = to rule. *Kyriarchy denotes the power to dominate of those "gentlemen" with property and education—heads of state, slave owners, and heads of households. Kyriarchy can best be theorized as a complex pyramidal system of super- and subordination, of exploitation and domination.*

Because the term kyriarchy is more comprehensive than patriarchy, I proposed in the early 1990s that the analytical terms patriarchy[9] and hierarchy be replaced with the intersectional analytics of kyriarchy. The term hierarchy is often used to describe the pyramid of domina-

---

[7] For more on feminist political science, cf. Birgit Sauer, "Begrenzung und Entgrenzung des Politischen: Geschlechterforschung in der Politikwissenschaft," in *Genus: Geschlechterforschung, Gender Studies in den Kultur- und Sozialwissenschaften*, 367-401.

[8] Cf. Elisabeth Schüssler Fiorenza, *But She Said: Feminist Practices of Biblical Interpretation* (Boston: Beacon Press, 1992).

[9] Sylvia Walby, *Patriarchy at Work: Patriarchal and Capitalist Relations in Employment, 1800-1984* (Minneapolis, Polity Press, 1986), 5-69. The author understands patriarchy as a complex system of mutually-interrelated social structures. The various groups of kyriarchal relationships shift in the course of time and each leads to other new constellations at different times and in different cultures.

tion, although it only designates a segment of kyriarchy, since it originally referred to a sacral pyramid of domination. While patriarchy[10] is
rejected by some as an unhistorical, universalistic, and totalizing
concept, others see it as a theoretical concept that adequately expresses
the origins and continuation of the sexual, social, political, and ideological power of men and their violence against wo/men. Therefore, in
feminist theory the meaning of the term "patriarchy" is no longer limited to the power of the *pater familias* over his extended family, as it is
still often the case in the social sciences. Rather, the term is used to
name those social structures and ideologies of domination that have al-
lowed men to infantilize and dominate women in the course of history.
Because the term patriarchy is understood in terms of male-female
gender difference, gender difference becomes the primary form of
domination and repression. The difference between male and female
becomes a fundamental and essential difference in what it means to be
human. Such an essentialist notion of gender difference can take a
constructive turn if it is assumed that binary gender difference is not
biologically determined or divinely ordained, but is a social construct.
Such ideological constructions of gender difference support kyriarchal
domination and allow it to appear as natural and self-evident—not only
for men but also for wo/men.
In order to come closer to redefining the center of feminist analysis,
however, I believe feminist the*logy and theory must relinquish as its
theoretical framework the privileging of binary gender dualism in
which "sexual difference [determines] the horizons" of our thought
(Luce Irigaray). This is necessary, because, hand in hand with the
kyriarchal ideologies of gender difference, oppositional discourses of
femininity inculcate the idea that gender and race are essential categories by allowing gender difference and racial difference to seem "real"
and "ordinary." This is achieved when "biological differences" are
ascribed deep symbolic meaning for our lives, instead of making an attempt to "denaturalize" and demystify such differences as sociopolitical and religious constructs.
For this reason, I have attempted to conceptualize and theorize the
notion of kyriarchy as a primary analytical category for feminist theory
in such a way that it can comprehend the interlocking, intersectional,[11]

---

[10] For more on the discussion and definition of the concept, cf., for example,
Maggie Humm, *The Dictionary of Feminist Theory* (Columbus, OH: Ohio State
University, 1990), 159-161; Gerda Lerner, *The Creation of Patriarchy* (New York:
Oxford University Press, 1986), 231-243. Unlike Lerner, I am not interested in the
origins of kyriarchal domination, but rather in its development as a heuristic
historical category.

[11] On intersectionality, see Elisabeth Schüssler Fiorenza, "Introduction: Exploring
the Intersections of Race, Gender, Status and Ethnicity in Early Christian Studies,"
in *Prejudice and Christian Beginnings: Investigating, Race, Gender and Ethnicity
in Early Christian Studies,* (ed. Laura Nasrallah and Elisabeth Schüssler Fiorenza;

and interdependent nature of the various structures of domination and forms of oppression of wo/men as well as oppression based on race, class, gender, and ethnicity. Instead of postulating a dualistic structure of domination (man-woman), the oppressive system must be understood theoretically as a pyramid-shaped, politico-cultural structure of domination (kyriarchy), organized in pyramidal form according to gender, race, class, religious group, or cultural affiliation and other historical articulations of domination.

It is not simply "man," but the Western, privileged, and educated gentleman who has produced knowledge and scholarship and has insisted that only his interpretation of the world is true and correct. Knowledge is thus not only gendered, but also raced, Eurocentric, and determined by class. The universalistic and kyriocentric scholarly rhetoric of Western male elites not only upholds the dominance of the male gender, but also the status of the "gentleman," the "white father," or the "boss man" (as an African-American expression calls him) as the universal subject.

In short, it is not only the exclusion of privileged Western wo/men from democratic civil rights together with that of all other "nonpersons" (Gustavo Gutierrez), but also the ideological legitimization of gender, race, class, and cultural differences as natural or divinely ordained which must be thought through theoretically in critical feminist terms. Instead of understanding kyriarchy as an all-encompassing totality which feminists can only escape by leaping into the "beyond" or escaping to a liberated community, a feminist, political, and decolonizing the*logy attempts to articulate an "other," alternative theoretical space at the heart of democratic kyriarchy, from where it can name so-called anthropological differences as sociopolitical and religious structures of domination.

Such an alternative space to kyriarchy, which is at the same time utopian and already historically actualized, is to be imagined as radical democracy. John McGowan points to the possibility of such an alternative space when he speaks about the difficult—indeed even antithetical—relationship between democracy and capitalism, emphasizing that only an appeal to those political and ethical principles inherent in a society can guarantee pluralism and difference.[12] In kyriarchal, democratic societies and religions, democratic principles such as freedom and equality are not to be understood as rigid unchangingconcepts, but rather as dynamic concepts which evoke again and again new meanings in different contexts.

Minneapolis: Fortress Press, 2009), 1-23; Gabriele Winker and Nina Degele, *Intersektionalität: Zur Analyse sozialer Ungleichheiten* (Bielefeld: Transcript Verlag, 2009).

[12] John McGowan, *Postmodernism and its Critics* (Ithaca, NY: Cornell University Press, 1991), 220-280.

Democracy is best understood as a community of equals seeking as good a life as possible, or as the independent practice of equal citizens. Power is not defined in terms of command and obedience, but corresponds to the human capacity to join together with others and act in concert with them. Radical democracy respects the fundamental dignity and differentiated equality of all people as autonomous citizens who take part in communal decision-making and are fully empowered to make decisions about their own well-being. According to Hannah Arendt—who, however, did not question the Greek city-state's structures of domination from a critical feminist perspective—the *polis,* a word from which politics is derived, is the organization of the people as it arises out of acting and speaking together, and its true space lies between people living together for this purpose, no matter where they happen to be. "Wherever you go, you will be a *polis*": these famous words . . . expressed the conviction that action and speech create a [democratic] space between the participants.[13]

Such an understanding of feminism as both a sociopolitical emancipatory movement and a scholarly perspective based on the conviction "that wo/men are people" alludes to the phrase [from the preamble to the U.S. Constitution] "we, the people." If "we, the people" in English is translated in German into "we the people [*das Volk*]" in the singular, then the concept of "the people" has very modern valences. Especially for those in German-speaking countries, it recalls the racist connotations of the nationalistic concept of the *Volk* "of blood and soil." If we translate "we, the people" with "we the people [*die Leute*]" in the plural instead—that is, ordinary persons coming from many different places—then it echoes the postmodern radical democratic "equal dignity of the many," of which Hannah Arendt speaks.

Social and religious movements for emancipation have thus repeatedly claimed self-determination and full citizenship for all without exceptions. The various sociopolitical liberation struggles and emancipatory movements of the last few centuries which have espoused full citizenship for all, such as abolitionism, the wo/men's movement, the labor movement, and the struggles against colonialism, heterosexism, and anti-Semitism, have been motivated to action by this contradiction between democratic vision and kyriarchal reality, as have the struggles for freedom of speech, religion, conscience, and research. They draw on scriptural texts and cultural and religious traditions which demand justice, respect, peace, the recognition of human dignity, cultural independence, well-being, and the equality of all as normative and divinely ordained.

---

[13] Hannah Arendt, *The Human Condition* (Chicago: Chicago University Press, 1958), 198.

These movements are the public space where a political decolonizing the*logy (which must always be a feminist the*logy at one and the same time) must be active and take a stand if it wishes to remain true to its own agenda. It must accept its emancipatory feminist responsibility in the public spheres of society, university, and church if it intends to identify and critique the structures of exclusion and the mechanisms of dehumanization in modernity and to work towards a radical democratic society and church.

It is thus necessary to rewrite the history of modernity in a feminist and postmodern key as the history of radical democratic movements for emancipation by those who have been excluded from democracy because they were not considered to be fully human. It is the story of those who have sought to assert the "equal dignity of the many."[14] It should have become clear by now that when I speak of democracy I do not mean primarily a form of representative government, but rather a social, radical-egalitarian ethos, which does not remain determined by the anthropological framework of gender difference.

III. Christianity, Modern Discourse on Femininity and Colonialism

With the emergence of democracy in antiquity and modernity, which proclaimed the same rights and duties for all who live in a state—although a large portion of the population was excluded from exercising their democratic rights—it became necessary to argue why certain people, such as freeborn wo/men or slave wo/men, could not be full citizens with all the attendant rights and duties.

In contrast to the feudalistic privileges of particular classes, the European Enlightenment emphasized the equality of all persons *qua* persons, while insisting at the same time on the otherness and inferiority of subordinated persons based on their gender or race [15] and the image of femininity of the "white lady" which was shaped by racism and colonialism. The ethos of "true femininity," of romantic love and domesticity, defined the essence of the middle-class woman as "being for others," which she had to live in and through actual or spir-

---

[14] Feminist the*logy as intercultural discourse has been formulated especially by Kwok Pui-Lan, "Feminist Theology as Intercultural Discourse," in *The Cambridge Companion to Feminist Theology,* (ed. Susan Frank Parsons; Cambridge: Cambridge University Press, 2002), 23-39.

[15] For a discussion of the affinity between fascism and thinking in terms of race, see especially Paul Gilroy, *Against Race: Imagining Political Culture Beyond the Color Line* (Cambridge: Harvard University Press, 2001). For more on the right-leaning, conservative tendencies of the "biologizing process" of femininity in fascism, cf., for example, *When Biology Became Destiny: Women in Weimar and Nazi Germany,* ed. Renate Bridenthal, Antina Grossmann and Marion Kaplan (New York: Monthly Review Press, 1984).

itual motherhood. The cultural socialization of wo/men geared towards selfless femininity and feminine relationality-work is perpetuated and codified through the division of labor in society and the Christian preaching of self-sacrificing love and humble service.

As a kyriarchal discourse, this discourse of femininity also continues to work in and through the theories about inferior races or "noble savages." The Enlightenment defined not only white wo/men, but also all other societal "non-persons" as "other," as natural beings who lack the characteristics to be fully human. The influence of this bourgeois discourse of femininity on the understanding and role of bourgeois religion is often overlooked. Since the Industrial Revolution and Enlightenment, religion in Europe and America has been removed from the public sphere and relegated to the private sphere of individualistic piety, charitable activity and the maintenance of culture, home, and family. Thus, the Christian churches as well as bourgeois wo/men (ladies) had a large stake in maintaining public interest in the antithetically understood "other" and in shaping social, national identity.[16]

Like the "White Lady," Christianity as a "missionary" religion had the task of "cultivating" the "savages," who were seen as "untamed nature." In this way, the Western discourses of femininity and "woman's nature" went hand in hand with the exercise of colonial power.[17] Theories and the*logies that absolutize and universalize the Western discourse of domination in terms of sexual difference or the complementarity of the genders obfuscate the involvement of white privileged wo/men and religious institutions in kyriarchal domination, since both have served as civilizing channels for knowledge as a means of domination and for religious and cultural values.

In the course of the privatization of religion and the "feminization" of culture, the clergy lost its privileged position in society and became more and more strongly in the political public equated with society ladies. At the same time, this feminization of religion has emphasized the political servant role of the church. It has led to the de-masculinization of the clergy in society[18] and, the intensified reassertion of the

---

[16] See, for example, Joan Jacobs Brumberg, "The Ethnological Mirror: American Women and Their Heathen Sisters, 1870-1910," in *Women and the Structure of Society: Selected Research from the Fifth Berkshire Conference on the History of Women*, ed. Barbara J. Harris and JoAnn K. McNamara (Durham, N.C.: Duke University Press, 1984), 108-128.

[17] See my article "The Politics of Otherness: Biblical Interpretation as a Critical Praxis for Liberation," in *The Future of Liberation Theology: Essays in Honor of Gustavo Gutiérrez*, (ed. Marc H. Ellis and Otto Maduro; Orbis: Maryknoll, NY, 1989), 311-325; and Kwok Pui-lan, "The Image of the 'White Lady': Gender and Race in Christian Mission," in Carr and Schüssler Fiorenza, *The Special Nature of Women?*, 19-27; See also Kwok Pui-lan, *Chinese Women and Christianity, 1860-1927*, American Academy of Religion Academy Series (Atlanta: Oxford University Press, 1992).

[18] Rosemary Radford Ruether, "Male Clericalism and the Dread of Women," *The

clergy's masculine role of dominance in the*logy, church, and family. Here the bitter debates over the ordination of wo/men, homosexuality, and the the*logical insistence on the "masculinity" of Jesus have their modern *Sitz im Leben*.[19]

This is also probably one of the main reasons why the new political the*logy, as well as postcolonial and liberation the*logies, have had difficulties in thinking critically about the entanglement of sexism, racism, heterosexism, classism, and nationalism in modern academic, ecclesiastical, and theological discourses. Johann Baptist Metz, for example, has argued that modern secularization processes are turning out more and more to be "processes of the disempowerment and dissolution of human beings as we have known them and been responsible for them."[20] But he does not take into account the critical feminist voices who have demonstrated that this human being "as we knew him" was one and the same as the white European master.[21]

Furthermore, Metz seeks to replace the death of God and the death of the subject announced by Nietzsche and postmodernity with the alternative articulation the "Enlightenment in the horizon of God remembrance," in order to resist the "vanishing of the human" and to save its "desire for self-determination" and "capacity for politics."

This argument, however, does not confront the feminist and postcolonial critical challenge to the biblical understanding of God and its instructions of domination and subordination,; remains silent about the horrible injustice "that cries out to heaven" [*himmelschreiende Ungerechtigkeit*] perpetrated in the name of the biblical God against wo/men and other people at the margins,; and forgets that the the*logical definition of the Other, of wo/men, homosexuals, heretics, savages, heathens, Jews—to name just a few concrete examples—was based on biblical-the*logical arguments. These still serve to reinforce the understanding of those who have been excluded as inferior, subordinate, and dependent and to justify taking away their freedoms and withholding justice. If political the*logy wishes to save the humanity and human dignity threatened by postmodern globalization,

---

Economist 11 (1973), 65-69.

[19] Cf. the analysis of this situation in my plenary address at the Second Ordination Conference 1978, reprinted in *Discipleship of Equals: A Critical Feminist Ekklesialogy of Liberation* (New York: Herder & Herder, 1993), 129-150, esp. 140-144. For an ecumenical comparison, see also Jacqueline Field-Bibb, *Women towards Priesthood: Ministerial Politics and Feminist Praxis* (New York: Cambridge University Press, 1991).

[20] Johann Baptist Metz, "Wider die zweite Unmündigkeit: Zum Verhältnis von Aufklärung und Christentum," in *Die Zukunft der Aufklärung*, 81.

[21] Cf. Cornelia Klinger, "Feministische Theorie zwischen Lektüre und Kritik des philosophischen Kanons," in *Genus: Geschlechterforschung/Gender Studies in den Kultur- und Sozialwissenschaften*, (ed. Hadumod Bussmann and Renate Hof;Stuttgart: Alfred Kröner Verlag, 2005), 329-364.

then then, in line with a critical feminist liberation the*logy, it must acknowledge as structural sin the damage that has been caused or enabled by the church and by the legacy of the biblical heritage about G*d, and it must self-critically acknowledge its own complicity in it.

IV. Postmodern Challenges to the Feminist Liberation Model

Andrea Günter, who was one of the first to encourage discussions between feminist the*logy and postmodern thought in the German-speaking world, nevertheless energetically called into question the approach of critical feminist liberation the*logy. She argues that the emancipatory model of a feminist the*logy conceived of as liberation the*logy should be rejected for the following reason:

> Behind such a generalizing model of victimhood and liberation there is an understanding of freedom, happiness, and the life of women which assumes that a woman must not only first become something—namely, free—but that the world itself must become altogether different. As a result this conveys that just like the world, so also a woman is nothing as she is, and that she must become something quite different before she obtains value and importance and can achieve "feminine freedom"—a judgment which contradicts the sense of life and self-worth of most women.[22]

While I agree with Günter's criticism of the victimhood model,[23] her equation of victimhood and liberation models seems to confuse several levels of analysis. A critical political and decolonizing the*logy works with a model of liberation that insists not only on an analysis of the structures of oppression, but also on the power and autonomy of the "non-persons" [*Untermenschen*] to engage in their own struggles against these structures. Such a liberation model works with the liberation-theological concept of structural sin exactly because feminist the*logy seeks to empower wo/men not to interpret situations of injustice, such as rape, as due to personal failings. To speak of structural sin does not mean that a woman or the world "is nothing as she (or it) is." Rather, because a concrete woman is socially as she is—namely a second- or third-class human being—she must be intent to change the world and herself if she wants to attain full self-determination.

Precisely in order not to see oppressive relationships as "given" and internalize them as negative sense of self-worth, oppressed people—men

---

[22] Andrea Günter, ed., *Feministische Theologie und postmodernes Denken: Zur theologischen Relevanz der Geschlechterdifferenz* (Stuttgart: Kohlhammer, 1996), 57.

[23] See the excellent analysis by Regula Strobel, *Opfer: Auseinandersetzung mit einem vielschichtigen Begriff und seinen problematischen Konsequenzen aus feministischer Perspektive*, Olympe: Feministische Arbeitshefte zur Politik 29 (2009) 89-98.

as well as wo/men—need a critical analysis of liberation which does not interpret "appalling injustice" the*logically as the will of God, but can name it as structural sin. This does not mean that wo/men are to be understood solely as victims. Wo/men as well as men are always also agents at one and the same time, which means they are also perpetrators. As the history of slavery and missionary colonialism teaches us, wo/men can very much dominate other wo/men or become the exploited victims of other wo/men, because wo/men just like men are always embedded in kyriarchal structures of domination and either collaborate with them or seek to change them.

As I have tried to show here, the modern academy and the*logy have articulated not only the "man of reason," but also the racist, colonialist ideology of femininity, that is, the essence of the "white lady," insofar as they understand the white lady as transmitter of culture and religion. European and American theories and the*logies, which absolutize and universalize the Western discourse of domination on gender difference, conceal the involvement of white privileged wo/men and Christian churches in the kyriarchal exercise of domination, because they have served as civilizing channels of both knowledge as a means of domination as well as of religious and cultural values.

This elucidates that emancipatory discourses are not independent from the dominant discourses of their kyriarchal societies, churches, and academic institutions in which they operate. On the contrary, they are inescapably entangled in these discourses of domination insofar as they have been conditioned by them. Hand-in-hand with the dominant ideologies of difference, theological discourses inculcate that gender and race are "natural" categories, because they allow gender and racial difference to appear as common sense.

Instead of universalizing the attributes of the white privileged Lady either as an object of research or as an academic subject, a critical feminist political the*logy of decolonizing liberation attempts to create as an alternative imaginative space a discursive forum where theological discourses can contribute towards transforming standardized, kyriarchal identity formations into creative difference and accordingly work out political strategies for a multi-voiced and multi-layered political feminist the*logy.

In order to articulate political-theologically such a critical, alternative space to the discourse of kyriarchy I have coined the concept of the *ekklēsia of wo/men*. Historically and politically, the term *ekklēsia of wo/men* is an *oxymoron*, that is, it is a combination of contradictory terms that seeks to articulate a political "Other." Because *ekklēsia* is qualified by the genitive "of wo/men," which refers to all non-citizens of modernity, this expression seeks to raise public awareness that neither church nor democracy is what they purport to be: *ekklēsia*, that is, the radical democratic congress of self-determining citizens.

Such a theoretical framework seeks to replace the exploitative construct of Woman as the Other of Man, or of a "black" or "savage" as the Other of "white" or "civilized" European, with the radical democratic construct of *ekklēsia*, which denotes both an as yet unfulfilled vision and a historical reality. The term does not delineate narrow identity boundaries, but rather unites the social and religious spheres, the single/individual/ group and the global movement. *Ekklēsia of wo/men* is always constituted where people come together to articulate and discuss their problems, visions, and goals and to celebrate them, as well as to make decisions together about strategies and means towards political and religious self-determination. *Ekklēsia of wo/men* emphasizes that wo/men and other *non-persons* are such autonomous citizens. *Ekklēsia of wo/men* is both already a reality and in the process of being realized.

The political tension between *kyriarchy* and *ekklēsia* not only orients *ekklēsia* towards changing kyriarchal church and society. It also maintains the awareness that the church is not a community of the liberated, but rather participates in both kyriarchal oppression and the reality of a liberated world towards which it is moving.

To conclude: A critical feminist the*logy of decolonizing liberation seeks to understand the *ekklēsia of wo/men* as an imaginative space where it can reflect on political, cultural, and religious change and can advocate radical democratic well-being. In so doing, such a feminist the*logy is critically aware that its social vision and analysis of liberation is shaped by the West. Nevertheless, it is not only relevant for European and American people but seems more and more necessary in the context of capitalist globalization around the world.

Photo © Stefan Kresin. Used by permission.

Francis Schüssler Fiorenza

Prospects for Political Theology
in the Face of Contemporary Challenges

In Germany during the 1960s a new political theology emerged as a critical reflection upon past theological conceptions of the relation of religion and society.[1] Jürgen Moltmann's *Theology of Hope* was a stunning breakthrough in relation to both dominant theologies of the day, especially Bultmann's existential interpretation of the Christian message. Johann Baptist Metz explicitly advocated a Political Theology in contrast to Karl Rahner's transcendental theology. Dorothee Sölle appealed to political theology as a political hermeneutic. These theologians began to advocate a new political theology two decades after World War II and during a time of strong economic development and national renewal. Within the postwar context, they critically reflected upon the recent German experience of National Socialism, the horrors of the war, and the Holocaust. At the same time, they brought to consciousness that the economic growth within a market economy not only made the market itself central to society, but also led increasingly to religion becoming a consumer object, often reduced to private individual choice.

These emergent political theologies criticized transcendental and existential theologies as inadequate to this situation. Not only did they fail to criticize the privatization of religion, but they even accentuated it through their emphasis upon the existential and upon individual decision. In contrast, the emergent political theologies offered a political hermeneutic of the Christian message, underscoring the centrality and reality of the promise of God's Kingdom. This proclamation required an eschatological, societal, and political horizon rather than an existential or transcendental one. As these theologians further articulated the themes of political theology in the following decades, they broadened and shifted its interpretive focus. Metz spelled out the significance of

---

[1] For a history of the concept of political theology, Francis Schüssler Fiorenza, "Religion und Politik: Geschichte und Funktion der politischen Theologie," in *Christlicher Glaube in moderner Gesellschaft*, vol. 27, eds. Karl Rahner and Bernhard Welte (Freiburg: Herder, 1982), 59-101. See also Ernst Feil, "Von der Politischen Theologie zur Theologie der Revolution," in *Diskussion zur Theologie der Revolution*, eds. Ernst Feil and Rudolf Wehr (München: Kaiser, 1969), 110-132, with a different assessment of its relation to liberation theology.

the memory of the passion of Jesus and the suffering of victims. He developed the category of "interruption" in contrast to progressive interpretations of history. Moltmann explicated the centrality of the crucified God and the Christian belief in the Trinity and also highlighted the relation of the belief in creation with ecological themes. Influenced by these theologians, Latin American liberation theologians (some educated in Europe) sought from the very beginning to differ from political theologians in their interpretation of the context, themes, and consequences.[2] They emphasized that their context was not the situation of secularization and privatization of religion, but one of economic dependency (buying somewhat into André Frank's dependency theory)[3] and the sharp contrast between the elites and the poor.[4] The liberation theologians argued that religion was not privatized as in modern Western Europe but that the church still had considerable influence. Therefore, they took issue not so much with transcendental or existential theology as with the previous liberal theological understanding of the church's mission and its consequences for social thought.

The distinction between hierarchy and laity was developed in the nineteenth century by Félicité Lamennais into a liberal notion of a public sphere as the sphere of the laity. This notion became dominant in Catholic theology in pre-Vatican II decades primarily through Yves Congar's understanding of the lay apostolate in the world. It posited a distinction of planes within the understanding of the church's mission: The primary task of the hierarchy was to preach the Gospel message, whereas the laity was concerned within the world.[5] That distinction actually developed the result of liberal Roman Catholic social thought that sought to counter the political integralism of a more controlling or interventionist role of the church's hierarchy within political society.[6] This liberalism within modern Catholic social thought suggested that the Christian messages to the social and political world be mediated through a rational and natural law.[7] In addition, Latin American the-

---

[2] Gustavo Gutiérrez, *A Theology of Liberation: History, Politics, and Salvation,* rev. ed. (London: SCM Press, 2001).

[3] André Gunder Frank, *Capitalism and Underdevelopment in Latin America* (New York: Modern Reader Paperbacks, 1969).

[4] Francis Schüssler Fiorenza, "Political Theology and Latin American Liberation Theologies," in *Modern Christian Thought: The Twentieth Century,* eds. Francis Schüssler Fiorenza and James Livingston (Minneapolis, MN: Augsburg Fortress, 2006) 273-308.

[5] Yves Congar, *Jalones pour une théologie du laïcat* (Paris: Editions du Cerf, 1953); idem, *Lay People in the Church: A Study for a Theology of Laity* (Westminster, MD: Newman, 1965).

[6] See Gutiérrez, *A Theology of Liberation* for his critique of the distinction of planes in relation to Congar's work and the mixed formulations of Vatican II in *Gaudium et spes.*

[7] Gutiérrez applies this criticism especially to Jacques Maritain, *Man and the State* (London, Hollis & Carter, 1954).

ology offered a more incarnational interpretation of eschatology that advocated the need for more historically concrete political options than the emphasis on eschatological proviso in political theology provided. In addition, as liberation theology developed, many focused much more on indigenous resources in native narratives and spirituality.

This brief and sketchy contrast between German Political Theology and Latin American Liberation Theology serves to profile the context and issues of political philosophy and theology within the United States—a profile differing from both Germany and Latin America. Although the reduction of religion to the private sphere within a market economy is to some extent operative, the public exercise and political influence of religion has increasingly taken on new roles in the public sphere. In addition, the process of globalization not only of the market, but also of travel and information brings issues of pluralism and difference to the fore and not only that of commodification. The differences call for a different articulation of political theology.

Nevertheless, to relate political theology to the context of the United States with its specific intellectual, political, economic and historical horizons is a rather complex endeavor.[8] Any interpretation of context and milieu remains controversial. Any move from theory to practice and from theology to practice is not unambiguous. Articulations of Christian beliefs and doctrines do not *eo ipso* implicate specific concrete political action. Likewise, any move from practice or from an interpretation of a specific context to a specific theoretical theological affirmation is open to debate. The challenge, however, remains: how does one articulate a political theology with the theoretical and political practice of the United States context? How does political theology engage with the practices and experiences of its context? This paper seeks to narrow that question to one particular phenomenon: the contemporary reemergence of Carl Schmitt's political theory and theology.

I. The Contrasting Functions of Carl Schmitt's Ideas

In the Anglo-Saxon world, there has been an increased theoretical in-

---

[8] Although the interest in Carl Schmitt extends to the Anglo-Saxon world, the US context is different in two ways. First, there was a specific justification of the war on terror within the Bush administration that mirrors the thought of Schmitt. Moreover, in regard to cultural homogeneity, the issues are reflected differently in the US than in Canada, for example, the immigration debates in the US and the multicultural issue in Canada in relation to the French-speaking areas. The latter has led to the development of strong multicultural political theories such as the work of Kymlicka. See Will Kymlicka, *Liberalism, Community, and Culture* (New York: Oxford University Press, 1989); idem, *The Rights of Minority Cultures* (New York: Oxford University Press, 1995); idem, Bashir Bashir, *The Politics of Reconciliation in Multicultural Societies* (New York: Oxford University Press, 2008).

terest in Carl Schmitt and his understanding of the "political," his critique of liberalism, and his political theology. Since the 1980s and 1990s, many of Carl Schmitt's writings have been translated into English: In 1985, both *Political Theology* and *The Crisis of Parliamentary Democracy*[9] appeared and they were followed one year later by *Political Romanticism*.[10] The next decade saw the translation of *The Concept of the Political* (1996), *Roman Catholicism and the Political Form* (1996), *Leviathan in the State Theory of Thomas Hobbes* (1996).[11] These were soon followed by *Land and Sea* (1997), and in the new millennium by *The Nomos of the Earth* in 2003, and *Constitutional Theory and Political Theology II* in 2008.[12] In addition to the translation of so many of his works, the secondary literature on Schmitt documents the considerable academic debate about the role of Schmitt's political theory.[13]

In the United States, however, Carl Schmitt's ideas have extended beyond any intellectual or academic engagement with his philosophy: they have been especially operative in political practice and governmental decisions. Former President George W. Bush's decisions and policies betrayed this influence in his advocacy of preemptive war, his disregard of international conventions such as the Geneva Conventions in regard to the treatment of prisoners of war, and his unilateralism in relation to the United Nations as well as to the system of International Court and Law. The Bush administration advocated policies and practices under the rubric of exception, emergency, and sovereignty that could be considered exemplifications of Carl Schmitt's thought. Moreover, there arose a sharp debate about the role of Leo Strauss's students within high levels of the Bush Administration.[14] Where

---

[9] Carl Schmitt, *Political Theology: Four Chapters on the Concept of Sovereignty* (Cambridge, MA: MIT Press, 1985); idem, *The Crisis of Parliamentary Democracy* (Cambridge, MA: MIT Press, 1985).

[10] Carl Schmitt, *Political Romanticism* (Cambridge, MA: MIT Press, 1986).

[11] Carl Schmitt, *The Concept of the Political* (Chicago: University of Chicago Press, 1996); idem, *The Leviathan in the State Theory of Thomas Hobbes* (Westport, Conn.: Greenwood Press, 1996); idem, *Roman Catholicism and Political Form* (Westport, Conn.: Greenwood, 1996).

[12] Carl Schmitt, *Land and Sea* (Washington, DC: Plutarch, 1997); idem with G. L. Ulmen, *The Nomos of the Earth in the International Law of the Jus Publicum Europaeum* (New York: Telos Press, 2003); idem, *Four Articles, 1931-1938* (Washington, D.C.: Plutarch, 1999). Carl Schmitt, Jeffrey Seitzer and Ellen Kennedy, *Constitutional Theory* (Durham: Duke University Press, 2008); idem, *Political Theology, II* (Malden, MA: Polity, 2008).

[13] For a brief survey, see Jürgen Manemann, *Carl Schmitt und die Politische Theologie: Politischer Anti-Monotheismus* (Münster: Aschendorff, 2002) 201-221. In addition, for the European reception, see Jan-Werner Müller, *A Dangerous Mind: Carl Schmitt in Post-War European Thought* (New Haven: Yale University Press, 2003).

[14] See James Atlas, The Nation: Leo-Cons: A Classicist Legacy: New Empire Builders, *The New York Times, Week in Review* May 4, Sect. 4: 1 Col. 3. Alan Frachon and Daniel Vernet, "The Strategist and the Philosopher: Leo Strauss and

Strauss is known for his critique of modernity and liberalism, there are significant differences between Carl Schmitt and Leo Strauss, his student.[15] In my opinion the decisive point is, however, the relation between the ideas of Carl Schmitt and the policies of the Bush administration. I want to be very clear and unambiguous about what I am claiming. I am not arguing for a causal relationship or direct influence of Carl Schmitt upon the Bush Administration—despite the presence of some former students of Strauss. Instead, I am claiming that there is a remarkable parallelism, if not correlation between the ideas and policies advocated by Carl Schmitt in regard to sovereignty, emergency legislation, preemptive war, and the disregard for rights and the ideas and policies that gained support within the Bush Administration in the wake of the destruction of the twin towers of the World Trade Center.

What is most interesting is that there are two very distinct, indeed contrasting roles for Schmitt's ideas. On the one hand, there is the role of his ideas within conservative political theory or neoconservative political policy and practice. On the other hand, there is the explicit retrieval and assimilation of Carl Schmitt within progressive or radical democratic thought, or, more precisely, within "agonistic political philosophy," as they self-designate themselves in their critique of liberal political philosophy.[16] This dual reception underscores the unique challenge to any contemporary theological reflection on the prospects for political theology today. It has to deal with the challenge of Carl Schmitt's political theology. That is not to say that German political theology did not seek to differentiate itself from Schmitt. After Hans Meier mistakenly mischaracterized Metz's political theology as a repetition of Schmitt's political theology, Metz sought to differentiate his political theology by characterizing it as a "new political theology" and by emphasizing the "memoria passionis Christi."[17] In addition, Jürgen

---

Albert Wohlstetter," *Counterpunch* (June 2, 2003); Shadia B. Drury, *Leo Strauss and the American Right,* 1st ed. (New York: St. Martin's Press, 1997), and Anne Norton, *Leo Strauss and the Politics of American Empire* (New Haven, CT: Yale University Press, 2004). For a critical review of essays of Norton, see James Costopoulos, "Anne Norton and the *Straussian* Cabal: How *Not* to Write a Book," *Interpretation* 32 (2005): 269-282, and David Lewis Schaefer, "The Ass and the Lion: Anne Norton, *Leo Strauss and the Politics of American Empire,*" *Interpretation* 32 (2005): 283-306.

[15] See Heinrich Meier, *Carl Schmitt and Leo Strauss: The Hidden Dialogue,* (Chicago: University of Chicago Press, 1995), and idem, *The Lesson of Carl Schmitt: Four Chapters on the Distinction between Political Theology and Political Philosophy* (Chicago: University of Chicago Press, 1998).

[16] Chantal Mouffe, *The Challenge of Carl Schmitt* (New York: Verso, 1999); idem, *Dimensions of Radical Democracy: Pluralism, Citizenship, Community* (New York: Verso, 1992); idem, *Deliberative Democracy or Agonistic Pluralism* (Wien: Institut für Höhere Studien, 2000).

[17] Johann Baptist Metz, *Memoria passionis: Ein provozierendes Gedächtnis in*

Moltmann developed the role of the crucifixion and Trinitarian theology with explicit reference to Erik Peterson's critique of political monotheism.[18] Furthermore, Carl Schmitt in *Political Theology, II* responded to both Metz and Moltmann's work.[19]

The reemergence of Carl Schmitt in contemporary discussions about political life is striking because it takes place in two simultaneous and contrary directions. It is not that there are two phases, i.e., first a conservative retrieval and then a radical democratic retrieval. Instead, these two retrievals contest one another. It is not like the transition from the presidency of George W. Bush to the presidency of Barack Obama that could be read as a transition away from a conservative to a more progressive politics.[20] There is, on the one hand, the obviously conservative or neoconservative retrieval of Carl Schmitt's theory. This reactionary return of Schmitt has taken place in both political theory and *de facto* in governmental practice, especially among the neoconservatives in the United States who dominated governmental political discourse and policy during President George Bush's administration and who still exist in the United States within the political as well as religious right.

Renewed interest in the theoretical positions of Schmitt's political theory and political theology has also taken place with a progressive direction; one might more appropriately characterize them as radical progressives to distinguish them from democratic or social liberals.[21] This direction of appropriation finds resonances in Schmitt's critique of liberalism. They are influenced by this critique not in order to return to the authoritarianism of Schmitt or even his own brand of fascism (which he represented before he switched to National Socialist fascism). Rather, they are influenced by the inadequacy of dominant political liberal philosophical thought, as represented by John Rawls, and to some extent Jürgen Habermas's discourse ethics and his understanding of the political, to which they extend their critique, though much less justified in my opinion.

---

pluralistischer Gesellschaft, ed. Johann Reikerstorfer (Freiburg: Herder 2006).

[18] See Jürgen Moltmann, *Der gekreuzigte Gott: Das Kreuz Christi als Grund und Kritik christlicher Theologie* (München: Chr. Kaiser, 1972); idem, *Trinität und Reich Gottes: Zur Gotteslehre* (München: Chr. Kaiser, 1980); idem, *Politische Theologie, Politische Ethik* (Mainz: Grünewald, 1984); idem, *On Human Dignity: Political Theology and Ethics* (Philadelphia: Fortress Press, 1984); idem, *Menschenwürde, Recht und Freiheit* (Berlin: Kreuz-Verlag, 1979).

[19] Carl Schmitt, *Political Theology, II* (Malden, MA: Polity, 2008).

[20] For the distinctive philosophical underpinnings of Obama's presidency, see the historical and philosophical analysis of James T. Kloppenberg, *Reading Obama: Dreams, Hope, and the American Political Tradition* (Princeton, NJ, Princeton University Press, 2011).

[21] For a general analysis of this position as "radical democratic," see Anna Marie Smith, *Laclau and Mouffe: The Radical Democratic Imaginary* (NY: Routledge, 1998).

II. Impulses within Neoconservative Political Thought and Practice

The neoconservative retrieval of Carl Schmitt's ideas has taken place in the wake of the events of September 11 and the collapse of the World Trade Center towers. It is this neoconservative movement that provided the intellectual resources for President George W. Bush in developing the theoretical foundations for some of his political decisions. One should recall that the very first sentence with which Carl Schmitt begins *Politische Theologie* affirms: "sovereign is the one who decides on the state of exception." In his political theology, Schmitt develops the notion that the state has a "monopoly of decision." It is not so much the monopoly of coercion or domination as it is the monopoly of decision[22]: the ability of the sovereign to decide in such a way that the sovereign is above what is legally constituted. The decision is, so to speak, created out of nothingness and the sovereign's power of decision relativizes the entire legal order. It was then the conservative position that affirmed it belonged to a unitary executive power to decide over the exceptional conditions.

It should be noted that there were considerable developments in Schmitt's conception of sovereignty, although these cannot be developed further here. What he wrote in his *Political Theology* and in *Concept of the Political* differs from what he wrote in 1922 or even as late as 1928 in his *Verfassungslehre*.[23] There is a move from a more Catholic to a more decisionistic interpretation of the political, and there is also a shift from a more Roman and classical understanding of sovereignty in his book on dictatorship in 1921 to an emphasis upon exceptional moments that require emergency measures and an emergency authority within his book *Political Theology*.[24] Moreover, there is considerable debate about the interpretation of Carl Schmitt, especially among those that view him primarily as a critic of liberalism rather than as a critic of democracy. By focusing on the critique of liberalism rather than on the critique of democracy, some are able to appropriate elements of his critique of liberalism and make that central to their reception. As a consequence, what Habermas, for example, finds objectionable and problematic about Schmitt—the separation of democracy and liberalism—is precisely what they find significant for their reception of Schmitt.

In examining American neoconservative political thought and practice in relation to Schmitt, there are significant aspects relevant to the war of terror even if one prescinds from its general neoconservative critique

---

[22] Carl Schmitt, *Politische Theologie*, 20.

[23] A shift takes place between Carl Schmitt, *Die Diktatur, von den Anfängen des modernen Souveränitätsgedankens bis zum proletarischen Klassenkampf* (München: Duncker & Humblot, 1921), and idem, *Verfassungslehre*, (München: Duncker & Humblot, 1928).

[24] There is this important shift between *Die Diktatur* and *Politische Theologie*.

of modernity and the Enlightenment. Bush's doctrine or slogan of "the axis of evil" underscored the friend/foe contrast insofar as he branded certain countries as evil and enemies, and others as friends and good. He established a governmental policy that should not officially negotiate with those nations branded as hostile. At the same time, he underscored the legitimacy of preemptive war or preemptive military strikes even if there was not the immediate or imminent danger of attack. In addition, the policy disregarded international law, especially the Geneva Conventions, with the explicit argument that the emergency situation in the wake of the attack on the World Trade Center justified torture in order to discover possible future threats. Then there was the importance of a cultural homogeneity in the face of the enemy and the general refusal to allow members of the United States military, even when present in other nations, to come under the jurisdiction of international law. These policies, attitudes, and acts should point us back to the context and reason for the development of human rights within the United Nations.

On December 10, 1948 the United Nations General Assembly accepted the Universal Declaration of Human Rights. This was the beginning of a set of declarations and covenants concerning rights. The immediate and driving context of the development of human rights after World War II was the memory of and reaction to the atrocities before and during the war. Several aspects of this post-World War II development of rights are important for political theology. The first is the specific memory of suffering that resulted from the rise of National Socialism and of the atrocities which took place not only in Europe but also in Asia. The other aspect represents the various covenants that elaborated a list of social rights urged by the developing countries and socialist nations. The United States has regrettably refused to sign many of these covenants and some were not even submitted to the US Senate for ratification lest it be obligated to alleviate the misery and poverty within the poor nations. These rights have, over the years, been expanded to include environmental rights especially insofar as the environment represents a global challenge.

The United Nations Charter itself and the various documents that constitute the International Bill of Rights should be interpreted as a response to the atrocities of World War II. The established limitations on "emergency" or "exception" legislation sought to hinder a repetition of the use of emergency legislation in Germany by the National Socialists. The Weimar Constitution (August 11, 1919) had Article 48: "If public safety and order in Germany are materially disturbed or endangered, the President may take the necessary measures to restore public safety and order, and, if necessary, to intervene with the help of the Armed Forces. To this end he may temporarily suspend, in whole or in part, the fundamental rights established in Articles 114, 115, 117,

118, 123, 124, and 153 paragraph 23." The legislation passed with the *Reichstagsbrandverordnung* and the *Ermächtigungsgesetz* later gave Hitler the power to protect the people and the state and therefore was in accordance with the emergency clause of the Weimar Constitution itself. The "emergency" of the burning of the Reichstag made it possible for the National Socialists to exclude basic rights and to give a juridical basis for a foreign policy that justified preemptive wars against alleged threats to security. Consequently, Hitler could claim a juridical basis for abolishing rights and for engaging in the preemptive invasions of France, Poland, Norway, and Denmark. The last chapter of *Mein Kampf* was entitled "als Recht" and Carl Schmitt issued his even before 1933.

The memory of these actions led the United Nations to contravene such unilateral appeals to exceptional emergencies. It thus underscored that collective and multilateral consensus was necessary for legitimacy.[25] David Little has suggested that the United Nations' documents can be seen as "Hitler's Epitaph."[26] However, these statements could just as easily have been seen as "Schmitt's Epitaph" though he lived long after the war. Article 51 of the United Nations Charter "internationalizes" the right of self-defense as does article 39 for collective security. The international and collective nature of legitimacy should prevent individual nations from declaring on their own that a situation constitutes an exceptional emergency situation that warrants the suspension of rights and preemptive attacks. The United Nations reinforced these safeguards through the fourth article of the International Covenant of Civil and Political Rights and through the Genocide Treaty because these limited what could be done in such exceptional cases of responses for the sake of national security.

Hitler had appealed to the singularity of an emergency to justify his action. Carl Schmitt appealed to the political theology of the French Restoration to argue that the power of the sovereign comes to the fore precisely in cases of exception and emergency. The response of the United Nations was not only to affirm the universality of human rights, but also to insist that appeals to emergency, exception, and preemption needed collective legitimation. In the face of the collapse of the World Trade Center, the President of the United States and the Attorney General of the Justice Department appealed to a similar rationale of "exception" and "emergency" and sought similar "exception legislation." There is a certain parallelism to their defense of the power of the President to act in such exceptional cases and Schmitt's theoretical and theological defense of a sovereign's exceptionalism. Hitler used the

---

[25] Johannes Morsink, *The Universal Declaration of Human Rights: Origins, Drafting, and Intent* (Philadelphia: University of Pennsylvania Press, 1999).

[26] David Little, "Liberalism and World Order: The Thought of James Luther Adams," *Harvard Divinity School Bulletin* 31 3 (2003) 7-9.

burning of the Reichstag in 1933 just as seventy years later in the wake
of September 11, the curtailing of basic rights took place in the name
of an exceptional emergency. The US Patriot Act allows the detention
of prisoners without warrants, public trials, or lawyers.[27] It curtails a
host of political and civil rights. Likewise, appealing to national
security, President Bush announced a policy of preemptive military
attacks, even in the absence of an immediate threat. In addition to the
enactment of "The Homeland Security Act of 2002," the debated
"Domestic Security Enhancement Act of 2003" (sometimes referred to
as "Patriot Act II") has further increased the powers of the Executive
Branch, especially the Justice Department and the FBI and abridged
political rights. The declarations by the Secretary of Defense that
certain prisoners were no longer subject to the Geneva Conventions led
to the abuse of enemy combatants and other prisoners. Such
declarations and actions violate the third of the Geneva Conventions
which was enacted to protect the rights of prisoners of war and the
fourth which was for the sake of civilians in the time of war.

These events show that the issues that Carl Schmitt's political theology
raised are still significant, not solely because of the increasingly historical interest in Schmitt's work within the United States,[28] but also
because of the present parallelism, if not a link, between the contemporary political argument that connects the exercise of presidential
sovereignty with emergency situations. It was precisely the use of sovereign power in exceptional situations that was the heart of Carl
Schmitt's political theology distinguishing a sovereign from an ad-
ministrator. As stated before, the beginning sentence of his *Political
Theology* reads, "Sovereign is the one who decides about the state of
exception."[29] George Bush gave his Presidential memoirs the title
Decision Points which recalled his own oft-repeated statement, "I am
the decider."[30]

At the origin of political theology stands not only an emphasis on the
state of exception, but also the sharp separation between friend and
enemy. Schmitt's political and constitutional theory rests on the sub-
stitution of *ethnos* for *demos*, of an ethnic grouping for a democratic
people. He underscored the cultural oneness of the ethnos in the face of
the enemy.[31] The former Attorney General of the United States, John

---

[27] The official title is: *Uniting and Strengthening America by Providing Appropriate Tools Required to Intercept and Obstruct Terrorism Act (Oct. 25, 2001)*, HR
3162 RDS.
[28] John P. McCormick, *Carl Schmitt's Critique of Liberalism: Against Politics as
Technology* (Cambridge: Cambridge University Press, 1997); see also, *Weber,
Habermas, and Transformations of the European State: Constitutional, Social, and
Supranational Democracy* (New York: Cambridge University Press, 2007).
[29] Carl Schmitt, *Politische Theologie*.
[30] George W. Bush, *Decision Points* (New York: Crown 2010).
[31] Ulrich Preuss, "Constitutional Powermaking for the new Polity: Some Delibera-

Ashcroft, responded as follows during a Senate hearing in December 2001: "To those who scare peace-loving people with phantoms of lost liberty, my message is this: 'Your tactics only aid terrorists, for they erode our national unity and diminish our resolve. They give ammunition to America's enemies.'" Similarly, President Bush divided the world into friends and enemies: those who are with us and those who are against us. It is George Bush's voice, but it reflects Schmitt's understanding of political sovereignty, his contrast between friend and enemy, and his advocacy of a homogeneous culture and people.[32] Such a viewpoint places his political theology, with its emphasis upon the importance of ethnos, in sharp contrast to any political theology that has a cosmopolitan view of the world of nations.

What has become clearer and clearer in the years since 9/11 is that the appeal to exception and emergency and increased demonization of enemies has had a devastating impact upon American actions. The title and subtitle of Jane Mayer's well-documented account expresses this well: *The Dark Side: The Inside Story of How the War on Terror Turned into a War on American Ideals*.[33] Likewise Tara McKelvey's *Monstering* documents show the American policy involvement with secret interrogations and torture.[34]

III. The Agonistic Appropriation of Schmitt

The agonistic appropriation of Carl Schmitt focuses on his understanding of the political realm and his critique of liberal political theory. In part, they concur with Schmitt's judgment about the decisive weaknesses of liberal political theory and liberal governance. However, instead of viewing Schmitt's authoritarianism and decisionism as a threat to the parliamentary democratic order, they argue it is only by taking Schmitt's critique seriously that one can advance a radically democratic society. What gives this radical or progressive appropriation of Schmitt a certain degree of popularity is the way it uses and combines Schmitt's critique of liberalism with other theories, often considered postmodern, such as Giorgio Agamben[35] and Jacques

---

tions on the Relations between Constituent Power and the Constitution," *Cardozo Law Review* 14 (1993): 639-660, here 650.

[32] See Carl Schmitt, *The Concept of the Political*. See the commentary on this work, Reinhard Mehring, *Carl Schmitt, Der Begriff des Politischen: Ein kooperativer Kommentar* (Berlin: Akademie Verlag, 2003).

[33] Jane Mayer, *The Dark Side: The Inside Story of How the War on Terror Turned into a War on American Ideals* (New York: Doubleday 2008).

[34] See *Monstering: Inside America's Policy of Secret Interrogations and Torture in the Terror War* (New York: Carroll & Graf, 2007).

[35] Giorgio Agamben, *State of Exception* (Chicago: University of Chicago Press, 2005); idem, *Homo Sacer: Sovereign Power and Bare Life* (Stanford, CA: Stanford

Derrida.[36] To some extent, what Klaus Tanner has affirmed for the early twentieth century could be affirmed today with one modification. "The point of Schmitt's argument is that he is consistent in channeling the widespread critique of the Enlightenment, Rationalism and Liberalism in the early twentieth century into a rejection of parliamentarism."[37] The modification today is that there is not so much a denial of parliamentary government as the claim that the current democratic forms are undemocratic.

In addition, this specific retrieval of Schmitt underscores the nature of the political as central to political and democratic life. In their view, current liberal political theory entails an eclipse of the political and in this sense they agree with Schmitt's critique of liberalism. Their agonistic theory of the political is an attempt to make the "political" central to political theory.[38] For example, in *The Return of the Political*, Chantal Mouffe has criticized the widespread view of John Rawls' theory of justice as a rebirth of political philosophy in the twentieth century. Instead Rawls' political liberalism if viewed seriously overlooks the nature of the political. What Rawls has achieved in this view is primarily a "mere extension of moral philosophy; it is moral reasoning applied to the treatment of political institutions. This is manifest in the absence in current liberal theorizing of a proper distinction between moral discourse and political discourse."[39] In developing this notion of the political they appeal to agonistic categories of difference, conflict, and hostility.[40]

By distinguishing Schmitt's critique of liberalism from his critique of democracy, they attempt to utilize his critique of liberalism as a way of advancing a much more radical democracy. In this way, as Mouffe ar-

---

University Press, 1998).

[36] For Derrida's analysis of Schmitt, see Jacques Derrida, *The Politics of Friendship* (New York: Verso, 1997; Original: *Politiques de l'amitié* (Paris: Éditions Galilie, 1994), especially chapter 5 that deals with absolute hostility. He considers hostility in relation to exception.

[37] "Der Punkt von Schmitts Argument ist, dass er die im frühen 20. Jahrhundert weit verbreitete Kritik an Aufklärung, Rationalismus und Liberalismus konsequent auf eine Absage an den Parlamentarismus richtet." Klaus Tanner, *Die fromme Verstaatlichung des Gewissens: Zur Auseinandersetzung um die Legitimität der Weimarer Reichsverfassung in Staatsrechtswissenschaft und Theologie der Zwanziger Jahre* (Göttingen: Vandenhoeck & Ruprecht, 1989), 57.

[38] See Bonnie Honig, *Political Theory and the Displacement of Politics* (Ithaca: Cornell University Press, 1993).

[39] Chantal Mouffe, *The Return of the Political* (London: Verso, 1993), 147. See also, *On the Political, Thinking in Action* (New York: Routledge, 2005). See also Ernesto Laclau and Chantal Mouffe, *Hegemony and Socialist Strategy: Towards a Radical Democratic Politics*, 2nd ed. (New York: Verso, 2001), and Ernesto Laclau, *The Making of Political Identities* (New York: Verso, 1994).

[40] See Noël O'Sullivan, "Difference and the Concept of the Political in Contemporary Political Philosophy," *Political Studies* XLV (1997), 739-754.

gues in the face of critics of her use of Carl Schmitt's political, she wants to use Schmitt against Schmitt. The critique of political liberalism underscores central ideas of Schmitt's understanding and critique of liberalism. One is the liberal appeal to neutrality which overlooks the conflicts of political life. It betrays the paradox of liberalism which contradicts the nature of political communities. The other is the accusation that liberalism with its appeal to consensus is rationalistic in its approach to politics. These criticisms circle around the failure of liberalism to acknowledge the significant role that power plays in politics. Instead of acknowledging the role of power, they substitute a reasonable consensus in political decision-making, thus failing to understand the very nature of the political. These criticisms bring Schmitt's criticism of the parliamentary democracy of the German Weimar Republic to bear in the North American discussions of John Rawls' political liberalism, as well as that of Ronald Dworkin and Timothy Scanlon.[41] Jürgen Habermas's work is often lumped together with Rawls, Dworkin, and Scanlon, which is not completely correct in my opinion. This recent introduction of Schmitt into the Anglo-Saxon world reminds one ironically that in 1986 in a review in the *London Literary Times* Jürgen Habermas noted that "Schmitt's philosophy will have no appeal in the Anglo-Saxon" world.[42]

Let me now briefly discuss each of these critiques.

IV. Critique of Liberalism and the Democratic Paradox

There is strong agreement with Schmitt's critique of liberalism as an approach to politics that tends to be much more procedural than substantive. In allowing for pluralism, it often relegates conceptions of the good as well as religious belief to the private sphere. It thereby overlooks the degree to which the political sphere is indeed the locus of struggles about the good. Schmitt argues that liberal democracy's fallacy is its attachment to the notion of public reason and its failure to see the distinct and incompatible norms that govern democracy and liberalism. Democracy advocates a self-sovereign society, whereas liberalism supports a pluralism that prevents the exercise of power by that self.

In a way that almost follows Schmitt's approach of criticizing liberalism by pointing out some of the very contradictions of liberalism,

---

[41] Ronald Dworkin, *Taking Rights Seriously* (Cambridge, MA: Harvard University Press, 1978); idem, *A Matter of Principle* (Cambridge, MA: Harvard University Press, 1985). Thomas Scanlon, *What We Owe to Each Other* (Cambridge, MA: University Press, 1998).

[42] Jürgen Habermas, "The Horrors of Autonomy: Carl Schmitt in English," in *The New Conservatism: Cultural Criticism and the Historians' Debate* (Cambridge: MIT, 1989).

Chantal Mouffe underscores the paradox of liberal democracy, namely, the nature of liberal democratic consensus and the nature of citizenship. What is the paradox of liberalism? On the one hand, there is the logic of liberalism that appeals to the universalism of human rights and underscores the more generic notion of humanity or the concept of human nature in general. On the other hand, there is the logic of democratic citizenship in which the sphere of the concrete political comes to the fore. The political needs to draw the boundaries of citizenship. It distinguishes citizens and non-citizens, friends and enemy. In this way Mouffe seeks to think with Schmitt against Schmitt. She draws on Schmitt to develop an agonistic position in contrast with what she calls the more rationalist or procedural approaches. The antagonist conceptions of a diverse group from William Connelly, Bonnie Honig, and Benjamin Barber want to include citizens' cultural identities that are based on groups.[43] Hence there is much more of an awareness of cultural, social, and ethnic differences than the more rationalist or consensus-oriented political theories suggest.

It is therefore suggested that "Schmitt can help us clarify what is at stake in this issue by making us aware of the tension existing between democracy and liberalism."[44] What is learned from Schmitt is the idea that the general equality of humankind cannot provide the basis for a specific government or particular state or political institution. Government is made possible by the possibility of distinction or difference. Schmitt argues in *The Concept of the Political*, "The political is the most intense and extreme antagonism, and every concrete antagonism becomes that much more political the closer it approaches the most extreme point, that of the friend-enemy grouping. In its entirety the state as an organized political entity describes for itself the friend-enemy distinction." The political government does not find its foundation in the equal identity or the "distinction-less-ness" of all people. Instead, it must be founded in a specific people.[45] The political involves the drawing of lines of demarcation and difference. It involves decisions that entail issues of power and values. Among these authors, there are obviously differences. Connolly argues for the "politics of paradox" and brings to the fore the "paradox of difference." Mouffe is concerned

---

[43] William E. Connolly, *Political Theory and Modernity* (New York, NY: B. Blackwell, 1988); idem, *The Ethos of Pluralization* (Minneapolis: University of Minnesota Press, 1995); idem, *Why I Am Not a Secularist* (Minneapolis: University of Minnesota Press, 1999). Benjamin R. Barber, *The Conquest of Politics: Liberal Philosophy in Democratic Times* (Princeton, NJ: Princeton University Press, 1988); idem, *Jihad vs. McWorld* (New York: Times Books, 1995).

[44] Chantal Mouffe, "Carl Schmitt and the Paradox of Liberal Democracy," *Canadian Journal of Law and Jurisprudence* 10 (1997), 21-33, here 22.

[45] It should be noted that Mouffe defends Schmitt from the charge of racism. The issue of his anti-Semitism is not taken as seriously as it should for its enduring relevance to his position.

with the paradox of liberal democracy. Both think that a pluralist democratic politics needs to expose paradoxes rather than transcending them through consensus or rationality.

V. Critique of Consensus and Challenges for Political Theology

The analysis of pluralism raises the question whether extreme pluralism as well as liberalism entails the "liberal evasion of the political." It was Carl Schmitt's view that liberalism was responsible for eliminating the decisive significance of politics for society insofar as the liberal neutralizes the political. Liberals such as John Rawls affirm that a liberal society needs a form of consensus that goes beyond a mere *modus vivendi* or mere procedural, but is based upon an overlapping consensus. Jürgen Habermas has objected in his extended exchange with John Rawls that such an overlapping consensus might serve the cause of stability but is insufficient for the sake of justification.[46] The agonistic philosophers object that Rawls' overlapping consensus would only be achieved in a "well-ordered society . . . from which politics has been eliminated."[47] Nevertheless, for the agonistic political philosophers both have avoided the issue of power. In this sense, they approach decisionism and, one could also say, nominalism with Schmitt's conception of sovereignty and the political.

The contemporary challenge of political theology is to examine the role that Carl Schmitt's political theology served in the 1930s and to ask— now more than seventy years later—how does one deal with today's crisis? Does it call for interruption, which is the center of Metz's political theology?[48] Does it call for "undecidability," as Jacques Derrida's political philosophy emphasizes?[49] Does it ridicule the universalism of rights with the label of "Esperanto," as George Lindbeck following Michael Walzer has done in giving priority to the local and particular?[50]

These questions are challenges one cannot answer easily. The emphasis on interruption and time in Metz's political theology and the emphasis on eschatology in Moltmann's understanding of human rights underscore not just the incompleteness, but also the distortions and injuries

---

[46] The dialogue which originally appeared in *Journal of Philosophy* has been printed in Jürgen Habermas, *The Inclusion of the Other: Studies in Political Theory* (Cambridge, MA: MIT Press, 1998), 49-101 = chapter 2 and 3; and John Rawls, *Political Liberalism*, expanded ed. (New York: Columbia University Press, 2005).

[47] Mouffe, *Cardozo Law Review* 16 (1995): 1533-1545. Here 1542.

[48] Metz, *Memoria Passionis*.

[49] Jacques Derrida, *Rogues: Two Essays on Reason* (Stanford: Stanford University Press, 2005); idem, *Politics of Friendship* (New York: Verso, 1997).

[50] George Lindbeck, *The Nature of Doctrine: Religion and Theology in a Postliberal Age* (Philadelphia: Westminster, 1984).

present in contemporary laws, institutions, and practices that are even enacted with an emancipatory intention. But one can at the same time also ask: Do today's international challenges and crises allow one to belittle international rights as an Esperanto?[51] Does not, instead, the international aspect of the challenge call for a more cosmopolitan vision? The destruction of the World Trade Center is indeed a quite different event from the burning down of the German parliament building [*Reichstag*]. Nevertheless, the use of "exception" legislation to weaken basic rights and to justify "pre-emptive" wars without imminent danger is formally very similar. Is there not a need for the further internationalization of rights and juridical means in the face of the many violations of rights that are caused within individual states by the states themselves or are the product of the negative impact of some economic capitalistic interests?[52]

Those who forget history are doomed to repeat it. Today we are experiencing a massive critique of human and political rights. It is striking that the political critique of rights relies in no small degree on the criticism of constitutionalism, of liberal democracy, and of "normativism" advanced by Carl Schmitt during the Nazi period. This critique of normativism has been taken up in part by his student Leo Strauss, whose own political philosophy, with its critique of modern liberalism, has had considerable influence upon the neoconservative movement in general, even if it is not as representative as some claim. Consequently, the current cultural and philosophical critique of human and political rights poses a challenge to political theology that raises anew the problem of the relation between political theology and political practice, between interpretation and action, between theology and human rights.[53]

VI. Neutrality, Civic Society, and the Modern Democratic State

A central point of Carl Schmitt's analysis of the modern democratic liberal state is the conflict or incompatibility between democratic principles and liberal principles. His analysis places principles of democratic procedures and liberal pluralism in competition and conflict with one another which many others would place as coequal or coconstitutive. Not only have the agonistic political philosophers made

---

[51] Michael Walzer, *Thick and Thin* (Notre Dame: University of Notre Dame Press, 1994), 9. In his later writings Walzer concedes a more universal but thin conception of rights.

[52] See the writings of Thomas Pögge, *Global Justice* (Malden, MA: Blackwell, 2001), and idem, *World Poverty and Human Rights* (Malden, MA: Polity, 2008).

[53] See Francis Schüssler Fiorenza, "Politische Theologie und liberale Gerechtig-keits-Konzeptionen," in *Mystik und Politik: Johann Baptist Metz zu Ehren,* ed. Edward Schillebeeckx (Mainz: Matthias Grünewald, 1988), 105 117.

this point central to their analysis, Ernst-Wolfgang Böckenförde, a member of Carl Schmitt's circle of friends and associates,[54] has defended Carl Schmitt against his critics arguing that the enemy/friend distinction should be understood phenomenologically rather than normatively.[55] But, more importantly, he has argued that the modern liberal secular state presupposes and is based upon premises it cannot guarantee. This argument elucidates the central point of Schmitt's critique of liberalism and democracy. It has been adopted by Joseph Cardinal Ratzinger, now Pope Benedict XVI, in his critical analysis of democracy.[56] It raises the question of the relation among liberalism, democracy, and religion within the modern pluralistic state.

John Rawls' political theory of justice seeks to develop an understanding of justice that takes into account the pluralism of contemporary societies. Consequently, he proposes that political liberalism relies on political norms and principles that various and diverse members of a political state can accept. This entails, especially in the judicial and legal institutional order, eschewing or avoiding what Rawls' labels "comprehensive doctrines"—a somewhat vague notion that includes religious beliefs as well as metaphysical positions. He refers to them as "comprehensive doctrines of a moral and religious character."[57] It is, of course, John Rawls' further and somewhat debated claim—though in my opinion open to misunderstanding and in fact often misinterpreted —that citizens should exclude or bracket out their specific religious beliefs as well as their metaphysical views when reflecting on the basic political structures of their nation and when interpreting the constitutional essentials of their society in order to obtain a consensus about political institutions and political norms. It is a position that maintains that when people go into the voting booth they have to leave behind their religious beliefs.

In a recent lecture at a symposium on religion entitled "The Political: The Rational Sense of a Questionable Inheritance of Political Theo-

---

[54] See Reinhard Mehring, *Carl Schmitt: Aufstieg und Fall* (München: Beck, 2009) for his biographical treatment also of the later Schmitt and his interaction with a circle of students and associates.

[55] Ernst-Wolfgang Böckenförde, *Der Staat als sittlicher Staat* (Berlin: Duncker & Humbolt, 1978), pp.12-17. See also his essays on political theology, now in volume two of his collected essays: *Kirchlicher Auftrag und politisches Handeln*, vol 2. (Freiburg: Herder, 1989), 91-159.

[56] Joseph Ratzinger, *Demokratie in der Kirche: Möglichkeiten, Grenzen, Gefahren* (Limburg: Lahn, 1970). The volume contains an essay by Hans Maier. See also Michael Welker's treatment of the dialogue between Habermas and Ratzinger in the present volume.

[57] John Rawls, *Theory of Justice* (Cambridge, MA: Harvard University Press, 1971); idem, *Political Liberalism* (New York: Columbia University Press, 1993); idem, "Justice as Fairness," *Philosophical Review* 67 (1958), 163-193; and Samuel R. Freeman, *Collected Papers* (Cambridge, MA: Harvard University Press, 1999).

logy," Jürgen Habermas addresses the challenge of Carl Schmitt.[58]
Habermas now points to one aspect of Schmitt's critique of liberalism,
namely, the neutrality and lack of normativity within the public realm
of society and politics. Habermas wants to retrieve the importance of
the normative within the public but in line with his own discourse ethics. Hence the emphasis in the title of his essay on "the rational sense"
of what in Schmitt's political theology is questionable. He suggests
that Schmitt's orientation on the French Revolution and the French
Counter-Reformation was unable to understand how such normativity
could be present in a democratic public realm of popular sovereignty.
In addition to differing from Schmitt, there is also a nuanced difference
to Rawls. Habermas makes a stronger appeal for the presence of the religious in the public realm than John Rawls and he nuances his usual
and easily misinterpreted notion of translation. I quote from his response:

> I do want to save also the imperative character of religious speech in the public
> sphere, because I'm convinced that there might well be buried intuitions that can
> be uncovered by a moving religious speech. Listening to Martin Luther King, it
> does make no difference whether you are secular or not. You understand what he
> means.[59]

The final sentence in the oral presentation, as recorded on the Internet
site, notes that Martin Luther King was indeed understood and killed
for it. Although Habermas often refers to the necessity of religious
language being translated, his understanding of the translation of religious language into the public sphere is highly debated.[60] Here he ac-
knowledges that religious language can be understood by the other.
One understands what Martin Luther King meant and it led to his death.
The questions that Habermas's position raises are multiple. First, he
clearly does not have a foundationalist view of language so that claims
have to be translated into some metalanguage. Particular theological
traditions or religious communities may assume just this when they

---

[58] Jürgen Habermas, "The Political: The Rational Meaning of a Questionable Inheritance of Political Theology," in *The Power of Religion in the Public Sphere*,
ed. Judith Butler et al (New York: Columbia University Press, 2011), 15-33; also
in same volume *Dialogue: Jürgen Habermas and Charles Taylor*, 60-69. See
Habermas's essays in religion and the public sphere and toleration in Jürgen
Habermas, *Between Naturalism and Religion: Philosophical Essays* (Malden, MA:
Polity, 2008), and the basis of his position in his *Between Facts and Norms* (Cambridge: MIT Press, 1996).
[59] "Dialogue: Jürgen Habermas and Charles Taylor," in *The Power of Religion in
the Public Sphere*, 60.
[60] See the debates on this issue and especially Habermas's response in Jürgen
Habermas, *Replik auf Einwände, Reaktion auf Anregungen*, in *Glauben und Wis-
sen: Ein Symposium mit Jürgen Habermas*, eds. Rudolf Langthaler and Herta
Nagl-Docekal (Berlin: Akademie Verlag, 2007), 366-414.

presuppose that moral claims based upon "natural law" independent of historical or cultural interpretations of nature should not be viewed as sectarian or religious claims or even the claim of a particular religious community. Secondly, the discourse theory of ethics points to the communicative principle of mutual perspective-taking. Such a mutual perspective-taking should allow that religious language often embodies claims that the other can understand and perhaps respect or reject. The fundamental principle of language claims that it be understood by the other and there has to be a mutual perspective-taking.

These two points are developed with two other considerations. All citizens can use religious language in the public sphere, but when they do, "they would have to accept that the potential truth content of religious utterances must be translated into a generally accessible language before they can find their way onto the agendas of parliaments, courts, or administrative bodies and decisions."[61] With this distinction between the language of parliaments and courts and the language of nonofficial or informal public rhetoric, his position is actually very close to John Rawls, when Rawls is interpreted with more nuance than his critics allow. However, Habermas makes another point in which he provides a nuanced rereading of Schmitt's emphasis. Habermas affirms that not only does democratic secular discourse and the discourse of religious citizens stand in complementary discourse to one another, but so does the affirmation:

As long as religious communities remain a vital force in civil society, their contribution to the legitimation process reflects an at least indirect reference to religion, which "the political" retains even within a secular state. Although religion can neither be reduced to morality nor be assimilated to ethical values orientation, the public use of reason by religious and nonreligious citizens alike may spur deliberative politics in a pluralist civil society and lead to the recovery of semantic potentials from religious traditions for a wider political culture.[62]

Where it is not understood, it has to be placed in the perspective of the other. This perspective of the other may be another religious language because of the increasing diversity of religious traditions in contemporary society; it may be another philosophical tradition than one's own; and it may also be secular language where the perspective of the other demands it. One can note both historically and in contemporary society the increased ability and skill of religious traditions or communities to take on the perspective of the other tradition or community. It is a significant step in the development of democratic and pluralistic communities. The point of linking a political theology with communicative action and speech is not to appeal to an overlapping consensus,

---

[61] Habermas, "The Political," in Butler, *The Power of Religion in the Public Sphere*, 25-26.
[62] Ibid., 27-28.

as the agonistic position in reliance on Schmitt often argues, but rather
to look at religious exchange and communication as an important element with the political formation of a society. Such exchange gives
substance to society and enables its constitutional language to be reinforced through the way the diverse religions interact with one another
and in turn also with secular currents within a society.

VII. Critique of the Denial of Victims and Powers:
Agonistic Difference

This critique of neutrality refers to Schmitt and his Hobbesian views in
order to underscore that all political decisions involve some people
having power, while other people are losing power and some people
are becoming subordinate to others. It seems to me that this is where
political theology has the ability to contribute from its own resources.
It is not only that Habermas quotes Martin Luther King's prophetic
proclamation to the nation. But it is also an anthropology that includes
the notion of sin and the relationship between sin and power.

Take, for example, Jürgen Habermas's interpretation of the evolution
of modernity. That interpretation is located within the framework of
the Frankfurt School that combines Weberian categories and its conception of bureaucracy with a revisionist Marxist account of capitalism,[63] to which Habermas incorporates and revises elements of a sys-
tem-theory relation to Talcott Parsons and Niklas Luhmann. My point
is not to explore possible modifications of an analysis of modernity in-
debted to Georg Lukacs's Weberian reading of Marx combined with
system analysis.[64] Instead, my question is: How does such an analysis
take into account the Holocaust as an appearance of modernity? How
does such an analysis take into account the killing fields of Cambodia
or the genocide within Rwanda? The agonist reception of Schmitt (con-
tra Schmitt) underscores that politics often involves the inclusion of
some groups in power and the exclusion of other groups in power and
that political deliberation and decision making creates exclusions and
subordinations.

This presents a challenge to a political theology not only to recall the
suffering of victims but to bring into consciousness an anthropology
that is aware of sin. Now, of course, the classic political theology of
Schmitt and French Reaction underscored sin but used sin or original
sin as a basis for an authoritarian government and as a basis for an anti-

---

[63] Jürgen Habermas, *Theorie des kommunikativen Handelns* (Frankfurt: Suhrkamp,
1981).
[64] Such an analysis has its validity especially when it underscores the inadequacy
of Schmitt's interpretation of modernity which overlooks the development of bu-
reaucratic structures.

popular sovereignty program. Of course, such analysis or appropriation of sin in Schmitt's political theology is rather one-sided. It overlooks the degree to which authoritarian governments create victims and engage in genocides. In the centuries since the French Revolution, we have not only the excesses of the masses in the wake of the revolution on the streets of Paris, but we have the excesses of authoritarian governments. In addition, in line with the French restorative political theologians, Schmitt's political theology maintains that an authoritative state is necessary to counteract a sinful humanity.

The Christian religious tradition has a strong sense of human sin and human frailty. How this understanding of human nature gets translated into social and political practice poses an important challenge to political theology. Reactionary and restorative theologians explicitly developed a political theology that appealed to original sin and underscored the need for strong authority, the need for a strong monarchy in contrast to a democratic plebiscite. These same theologians, to whom Carl Schmitt appealed, also argued that a sovereign should not be bound by constitutions just as God was not bound by nature but could intervene with exceptions as in the case of miracles. The history of the twentieth century has shown that authoritarian governments have led to many of the atrocities within the twentieth century. The actions of some democratic governments can likewise be faulted.

The tasks of a political theology are both reconstructive and constructive. They are reconstructive insofar as they reconstruct how Christian beliefs and practices have affected historical practices. For example, one can see how anti-Semitic exclusions historically influenced a population's acceptance of more racially-based anti-Semitism in the twentieth century. One can also see how self-interest, not merely in the sense of survival or the *conatus essendi* but also in terms of the desire for power and domination, stands behind some of the political evils we face. There are elements of religious traditions with their concern for the other, for the disenfranchised, for the stranger, that underscore that the human self through its commitment to mutual respect, and human communities through their commitment to justice and its embodiment in law, work against the power within the human self and community to become instantiations in a set of structures that are hostile to others.

VIII. Rights and Transcendence in the Face of Exceptions and Exclusions

The previous challenge to political theology points to the necessity of taking the exclusions of the political seriously through its memory of suffering and through its awareness of sin.

Another significant issue is whether political theology as arising from

religious commitment brings a sense of transcendence that goes beyond the particularity of a nation. When the justification of emergency
measures, such as the torture of prisoners of war, is based upon the allegedly "greater good" of the survival of the nation, in this case the
United States, does not a religious belief in transcendence that goes
beyond the nation make a significant contribution? Many religious traditions often go beyond local, ethnic, tribal, or national political units.
Insofar as they do, these religious traditions present a horizon, place
limits, and serve as a criticism of a political theology focused on the
sovereignty and survival of the nation. In the twentieth century
advocates of human rights, especially through the United Nations Declaration of Human Rights, have sought to develop an understanding of
human rights in ways that can cross cultures and not be dependent
upon a specific religious tradition for their grounding. Such an attempt
is understandable in the face of the diverse religious traditions and diverse secular traditions within the world and therefore should be en-
couraged. But that does not entail that the individual religious traditions themselves elaborate how their religious traditions can contribute a religious understanding of human rights. They can offer
religious models and profiles of practice that exemplify these rights
even in the face of adversity. They offer an understanding of reality in
which the belief in God or the belief in transcendence overrides
national or ethnic interests when these are used as the basis for the disregard of human rights as in the example of torture, firebombing of
cities, even the use of atomic weapons.

IX. Summary

In this paper I have underscored how the ideas in Carl Schmitt's political theology and political philosophy are operative in two contrasting
directions: the neoconservative and the radical. In the face of the
Schmitt's political theology and the neoconservative appeal to a strong
sovereign who dispenses with universal notions of right and international law in cases of exception or emergency, I have pointed to the
historical consequences that have emerged from an emphasis upon exception in times of emergency. Such consequences underscore the importance of political theology supporting a strong conception of rights
and constitutional rights, rather than undermining them. In the face of
the appeal of the agonistic reception of Schmitt, I have argued for the
development of public religious discourse in which political theology
has to develop its approach to bring its values into the public sphere
either directly or by linking it with other discourses.
To the extent that public religious discourse in a pluralist society en-
gages in a mutual perspective, taking in relations to other religious

communities and secular tradition, it contributes to the formation of the democratic. In addition, a Christian political theology needs to articulate an understanding of human nature as sinful but not in order to justify the need for authoritarian governments to restrain the masses. Instead, theological reflection on the core beliefs of the Christian religious tradition needs to explicate their understanding of sin to uncover the power within the human self that leads to exclusions, repressions, and genocides, and it has to mobilize the religious traditions' concern for the other to work against such forces. Finally, the belief in transcendence, specified in the Christian tradition as God, provides a horizon that undercuts the self-interest of nations and can and should be mobilized to go beyond the friend/enemy dichotomy that is used by nations to justify the neglect of important human rights.

Photo © Stefan Kresin. Used by permission.

Klaus Tanner

Political Theology According to Benedict XVI

I.

Discussions about power are at the heart of all religious communication. In the processes of explaining and interpreting human existence subsumed under the category of "religion," experiences and images of power and powerlessness play a key role.[1] On the one hand, questions of power are raised with regards to the challenge of self-control. On the other hand, questions are also raised about the fundamental sociality of all human lifestyles. Since no one can live life alone, the classical subjects of religious communication necessarily include questions about how to coordinate and order communal life. In this sense these subjects always have a "political" dimension. In the history of Christianity and our culture, questions about how to regulate the order and constitution of collective life have always been strongly correlated with how Christians conceive of human forms of life.

This also applies to the specifically modern condition of the social differentiation between political and "religious" institutions. In his Geschichte des Westens, for example, Heinrich August Winkler pointed out once again how significant the "specifically Christian . . . differentiation between divine and secular order" has been in shaping our culture.[2] If it is true that the understanding of politics and Christian ways of conceiving of life have remained closely related in ways that are varied and replete with tensions, then it makes little sense to work with stark distinctions that dichotomize between "political" and "unpolitical" forms in which Christians interpret and live their lives. Some conflicts in the church and between theologies are less disputes between political and unpolitical positions than conflicts about differing

---

[1] See, for example, Paul Tillich, "Das Problem der Macht: Versuch einer philosophischen Grundlegung" (1931), in Tillich, Gesammelte Werke, vol. II (Stuttgart: Evangelisches Verlagswerk, 1962), 193-208; Tillich, Liebe, Macht, Gerechtigkeit (1954), in: Tillich, Gesammelte Werke, vol. XI (Stuttgart: Evangelisches Verlagswerk, 1969), 143-225; Gert Melville, ed., Das Sichtbare und das Unsichtbare der Macht: Institutionelle Prozesse in Antike, Mittelalter und Neuzeit (Cologne: Böhlau, 2005).
[2] Heinrich August Winkler, Geschichte des Westens: Von den Anfängen in der Antike bis zum 20 Jahrhundert (München: Beck, 2009), 19

understandings of the "political" dimension of Christianity's interpretation of itself and the world.

It also does not make sense to categorize the "new political theology"[3]
and the "classical" Catholic theologies of order in terms of the
distinction between the political and unpolitical, because even these
classical theories of order contain elaborate doctrines of the state and
social teachings.[4]

In what follows I wish to provide a brief overview of the encyclicals of
Benedict XVI, in order to tease out some aspects of this political dimension. This theological understanding of the political dimension of
Christianity's interpretation of itself and the world is centered on the
two concepts of love and truth. According to Benedict XVI, "love in
the truth"[5] is the decisive political power that is supposed to imbue and
shape the institution of the church as well as all forms of communal
life in state and society.

II.

After his election to the papacy on 19 April 2005, Joseph Aloisius
Ratzinger published his first encyclical, Deus Caritas Est,[6] in the same
year. Such communiqués from the Apostolic See are made in the name
of an authority that already has its own political relevance. This authority oscillates between spiritual and secular forms of authority, for the
Pope never speaks only as the Bishop of Rome: he is always the head
of the Vatican City state as well. This state is characterized by a strong
claim to sovereignty. The Vatican's form of government is an absolute
monarchy,[7] which maintains a diplomatic corps operating worldwide,

---

[3] Johann Baptist Metz, Zum Begriff der neuen politischen Theologie (1967-1997)
(Mainz: Matthias-Grünewald-Verlag, 1997).

[4] Cf. the depiction of Thomistic ethics and social philosophy as one of the most influential types of Christian ideas in Ernst Troeltsch, Die Soziallehren der christ-
lichen Kirchen und Gruppen (Tübingen: Mohr, 1912), 252-358. For more on German Catholicism after the French Revolution, cf. the very thorough academic study
describing the distinctions between central political themes in a multifaceted way
by Rudolf Uertz, Vom Gottesrecht zum Menschenrecht: Das katholische Staatsdenken in Deutschland von der Französischen Revolution bis zum II. Vatikanischen Konzil (1789-1965) (Paderborn: Schöningh, 2005).

[5] This is the title of the third encyclical letter of Benedict XVI, Charity in Truth:
Caritas in Veritate, Encyclical letter on integral human development in charity and
truth, Nr. 186, June 29, 2009. All references in this text include the paragraph
number. Quotes from the encyclical come from the official English version of this
text. It can be accessed online at the Vatican website: http://www.vatican.va/-
holy_father/benedict_xvi/encyclicals/ index_en.htm.

[6] Benedikt XVI., Encylica Deus Caritas Est, It is available online in English at the
Vatican website. See footnote 5.

[7] Cf. "Das neue Grundgesetz des Vatikanstaates" [The new Fundamental Law of

for which such doctrinal texts provide a binding basis for political activity.[8]

Deus Caritas Est was supposed to be a programmatic text which, at the beginning of Benedict XVI's pontificate, would lay down "basic elements" (DCE, Nr. 1) upon which the entire proclamation and praxis of the Roman church is built. For Benedict XVI, the central foundational element is an understanding of God in line with 1 John 4:16, which understands God as the acme of love. In the first main section this understanding of love is underlaid christologically and with a "strictly metaphysical image of God."[9] The second section develops the main features of an ecclesiology, according to which the church is the decisive expression and realization of divine love. Its social form is characterized as "God's family" (DCE, Nr. 32).

The use of the concept of love starkly separates the understanding of God from Greek philosophy.[10] The social and political dimensions are recovered through the connection between divine love and love for neighbor. The specifically Jewish and Christian understanding of God is based on the "ecclesial exercise of the commandment of love of neighbour" (DCE, Nr. 1). It is only possible with Christian "love of neighbor" to overcome "the selfish character" in humanity so there can be a "real discovery of the other" (DCE, Nr. 6). This implies that the church as "God's family in the world" must be a place where there is all-embracing mutual help, where "no one ought to go without the necessities of life" (DCE, Nr. 25).

A far-reaching validity claim is made for Christian love for one's neighbor: "the command of love of neighbour is inscribed by the Creator in man's very nature" (DCE, Nr. 31). This theological claim to

the Vatican City State], Acta Apostolicae Sedis Ergänzungsband 93 (2001), Art. 1.1: "As head of the Vatican City State the Pope possesses the fullness of legislative executive and judicial authority." See also CIC (1983 Codex Iuris Canonici) c. 331: "The Bishop of the Church of Rome . . . possesses . . . by virtue of his office in the church the highest, complete, immediate and universal regular authority, which he can always exercise freely." (Quote translated by translator of this article.)

[8] 1983 Codex Iuris Canonici [Canonical legislation for the Latin Rite of the Roman Catholic Church] cc. 362ff.

[9] "The philosophical dimension to be noted in this biblical vision, and its importance from the standpoint of the history of religions, lies in the fact that on the one hand we find ourselves before a strictly metaphysical image of God: God is the absolute and ultimate source of all being; but this universal principle of creation—the Logos, primordial reason—is at the same time a lover with all the passion of a true love. Eros is thus supremely ennobled, yet at the same time it is so purified as to become one with agape." (DCE, Nr. 10, italics in original).

[10] "The divine power that Aristotle at the height of Greek philosophy sought to grasp through reflection, is indeed for every being an object of desire and of love —and as the object of love this divinity moves the world—but in itself it lacks nothing and does not love: it is solely the object of love. The one God in whom Israel believes, on the other hand, loves with a personal love."(DCE, Nr. 9).

universality is also articulated in the goals of the encylical. It seeks nothing less than the "healing the whole human race" (DCE, Nr. 9) or rather, the realization of a "true humanism" (DCE, Nr. 30).

Given the claim to universality, these arguments, which at first appear to be focused on ecclesiological issues, are de facto closely related to a definition of the "central responsibility of politics" as the realization of "justice" (DCE, Nr. 28). Politics, however, cannot realize this task entirely on its own. It requires, as it were, an energy input, the "living forces" of the church, for "she is alive with the love enkindled by the Spirit of Christ." (DCE, Nr. 28).

The topic of Benedict XVI's next encyclical letter, published in November 2007, is hope. In Spe salvi[11] the fundamental characteristics of the Pope's interpretation of history are even more clearly recognizable than in Deus Caritas Est. This includes a massive critique of modernity. He outlines and then criticizes the transformation of Christian eschatology into an intraworldly faith in progress, providing examples such as the Scientific Revolution (especially Francis Bacon[12]), the French Revolution, and the Marxist and Communist "road[s] towards revolution" (SpS, Nr. 20). The Frankfurt School is offered as an example in support of his critique:

In the twentieth century, Theodor W. Adorno formulated the problem of faith in progress quite drastically: he said that progress, seen accurately, is progress from the sling to the atom bomb. Now this is certainly an aspect of progress that must not be concealed. To put it another way: the ambiguity of progress becomes evident. Without doubt, it offers new possibilities for good, but it also opens up appalling possibilities for evil—possibilities that formerly did not exist. (SpS, Nr. 22).

The third encyclical Caritas in Veritate appeared in July 2009.[13] In this social encyclical letter, which is explicitly aimed not just at Christians but "all people of good will,"[14] the pope takes up and expands upon the

---

[11] Benedict XVI, Encyclical Letter *Spe Salvi*, See footnote 5.

[12] In Bacon one sees "a disturbing step has been taken: up to that time, the recovery of what man had lost through the expulsion from Paradise was expected from faith in Jesus Christ: herein lay "redemption." Now, this "redemption," the restoration of the lost "Paradise" is no longer expected from faith, but from the newly discovered link between science and praxis. It is not that faith is simply denied; rather it is displaced onto another level—that of purely private and other-worldly affairs—and at the same time it becomes somehow irrelevant for the world. This programmatic vision has determined the trajectory of modern times and it also shapes the present-day crisis of faith which is essentially a crisis of Christian hope." (SpS, Nr. 17).

[13] Benedict XVI, Encyclical Letter: Caritas in Veritate. Available online at the Vatican website (see footnote 5).

[14] The complete title is: "Encyclical Letter Caritas in Veritate of the Supreme Pontiff Benedict XVI to the Bishops, Priests, and Deacons, Men and Women Religious, the Lay Faithful and all People of Good Will on Integral Human Development in Charity and Truth."

subject of love from his 2005 encyclical letter. The text is interspersed with appellative language in which he repeatedly calls for morally responsible action.

This communiqué of the Apostolic See was politically well timed. It appeared shortly before the meeting of the heads of government of the most important industrial nations (the so-called G8) in the Italian city of L'Aquila, which took place in the midst of the international financial and economic crisis. On his trip to Italy, the newly elected American president Barack Obama even found time for a meeting with the Pope.[15]

Guided by the central concept of "integral [human] development," the text is an update of Roman Catholic social teaching in the age of globalization. Benedict aligns his text with the major social encyclicals. What was begun with Rerum Novarum (1891) was continued in Populorum Progressio (1967) by Paul VI. This text by Paul VI—and not the texts of the Second Vatican Council—is the crucial reference point for Benedict XVI. The social encyclicals of John Paul II play a subordinate role. Benedict XVI largely affirms the content of Populorum Progressio.

Emphasizing a concept of history of salvation, Benedict claims a key competency for the church for the "development of every person and of all humanity" (CiV, Nr. 1) towards a true "humanism" (CiV, Nr. 16 and Nr. 18) or a "new humanistic synthesis" (CiV, Nr. 21): the development in its entirety is to be understood as a process whose purpose and goal lies in a "plan" of God; at the same time, "life in Christ is the first and principal factor in the development" of all humanity (CiV, Nr. 8). The goal is paraphrased in a highly metaphorical way as the "universal city of God" or "undivided city of God" (SpS, Nr. 7).

The central ethical reference point in the 120-page encyclical letter, in which a number of subjects related to political, economic and social development are addressed,[16] are the classical topoi of Roman Catholic social teaching of "common good" and "justice."

---

[15] The Pope explicitly presented his encyclical letter once again at a general audience held during the G8 Summit and attended by some of the "First Ladies" of the state leaders and heads of government who had come to the summit (cf. the German article: "Benedikt XVI. erläutert die Kernaussagen seiner dritten Enzyklika: Generalaudienz im Zeichen von Caritas in Veritate," Zenit 08.07.2009, online http://www.zenit.org/article-18231?l=german. Called up on 14.02.2012).

[16] The newspapers commented that this document was a "hodgepodge" [Sammelsurium] (according to Matthias Drobinski, "Der weltfremde Papst," Süddeutsche Zeitung, 8 July 2009) and a "Roman catalogue of problems that knows no bounds" or again "an inventory of items seemingly piled up on top of each other" (according to Uwe Justus Wenzel in "Sehnsucht nach einer 'echten politischen Weltautorität,'" Neue Zürcher Zeitung, 9 July 2009).

III.

In the positions he takes with regard to the problems of political and social order, Benedict XVI is referring back to a complex of issues which he as Joseph Cardinal Ratzinger, prefect for the Congregation for the Doctrine of the Faith, had already discussed intensively in his massive critique of the "theology of liberation" in the 1980s[17]. The reception of Marxist methods of social analysis in liberation theologies was sharply criticized in this document. This critique of Marxism is also a central theme in Benedict XVI's encyclicals. However, it remains at the level of sheer negation; there are no indications in the texts of an alternative methodological instrument for analyzing historical processes of change and societal development.[18] Instead, there are speculative and metaphysical modes of argumentation in which he reasons about the relationship between reason and love in an abstract way or calls for a "transcendent view of the person" (CiV, Nr. 11).

It should not be surprising that in this intellectual framework the true causes of these crisis developments are "not primarily of the material order," as Benedict XVI writes in keeping with Paul VI's encyclical letter Populorum Progressio (CiV, Nr. 19). In its interpretation of the contemporary situation, Caritas in Veritate deploys the entire classical repertoire of conservative cultural criticism. The causes of the crises are "ideologies" (CiV, Nr. 14), an "empiricist and sceptical view of life" (CiV, Nr. 9), the "increased commercialization of cultural exchange," "cultural levelling" (CiV, Nr. 26), "hedonism and consumerism" (CiV, Nr. 51), a "practical atheism" (CiV, Nr. 29), the "excessive segmentation of knowledge, the rejection of metaphysics by the human sciences" (CiV, Nr. 31), technocracy, and again and again cultural "relativism" or the "tendency to relativize the truth" (CiV, Nr. 4).

The decisive element that shapes and guides the processes of "integral" development towards the "universal city of God" (CiV, Nr. 7) are apparently supposed to be moral convictions, the "values of Christianity" (CiV, Nr. 4) or "fundamental values" (CiV, Nr. 21)—although he does not feel the need to discuss the institutional conditions impinging on the conveyance and implementation of such "values." The lack of social scientific analysis is reflected in a catalog of recommendations for

---

[17] Cf. the instruction by the Congregation for the Doctrine of the Faith issued under him relating to some aspects of the "Theology of Liberation." Available online in English at the Vatican website: http://www.vatican.va/roman_curia/congregations/-cfaith/documents/rc_con_cfaith_doc_19840806_theology-liberation_en.html.

[18] Cf. the criticism by Leonardo Boff, "The Pope Lacks a Bit of Marxism" from 17 July 2009, available online at http://leonardoboff.com/site-eng/vista/2009/-jul17.htm. Called up on 14 February 2012. Boff comes to the conclusion: "The dominant tone is not of analysis, but of ethics, of what should be." The magisterial statement "sticks to principles" and is "blithely out of and above the present conflictive situation."

the market, the state and the civil society, all of which remain very vague.[19] This becomes clear in the central themes of the encyclical letter, which is globalization or the "development of peoples" (CiV, Nr. 43 among others). This depiction ends in a call for a political world authority that needs "to be universally recognized and to be vested with . . . effective power (CiV, Nr. 67): "To manage the global economy; to revive economies hit by the crisis; to avoid any deterioration of the present crisis and the greater imbalances that would result; to bring about integral and timely disarmament, food security and peace; to guarantee the protection of the environment and to regulate migration, for all this, there is urgent need of a true world political authority." (CiV, Nr. 67).

IV.

The pope wanted his text to be understood as a contribution towards addressing fundamental questions rather than suggesting "technical solutions" (CiV, Nr. 9). At core it is just one task to which he wishes to draw attention: the understanding of reason and the necessity of "purifying" reason (CiV, Nr. 56).[20] The key proposition can be summarized thus: Without a theonomic foundation for human reason, development cannot be successful. A "broadening [of] our concept of reason and its application" is indispensable (CiV, Nr. 31, which references a lecture given at the University of Regensburg in 2006) through opening up the understanding of reason towards "transcendence" (CiV, Nr. 74). The de facto effect of these formulas is, first of all, an extensive critique of the modern understanding of reason which, according to Benedict reduces reason to a force to be employed for merely technical and instrumental purposes. Love must be linked with—even placed over—this reduced reason as the decisive divine force.[21] In a formula echoing Kant's epistemology of the dual origins of human knowledge, he writes: "Deeds without knowledge are blind, and knowledge without love is sterile. Indeed, 'the individual who is animated by true charity

---

[19] "What should be avoided is a speculative use of financial resources that yields to the temptation of seeking only short-term profit." (CiV, Nr. 40). Finance as such requires "renewed structures and operating methods" (CiV, Nr. 65).

[20] This question was already at the center of his controversial lecture in Regensburg, and was published as: Benedict XVI, "Glaube, Vernunft und Universität: Erinnerungen und Reflexionen," in Benedict XVI., ed., Glaube und Vernunft: Die Regensburger Vorlesung (Freiburg/Breisgau: Herder, 2006), 11-32.

[21] "Charity does not exclude knowledge, but rather requires, promotes, and animates it from within. Knowledge is never purely the work of the intellect. It can certainly be reduced to calculation and experiment, but if it aspires to be wisdom capable of directing man in the light of his first beginnings and his final ends, it must be "seasoned" with the "salt" of charity." (CiV, Nr. 30; cf. also Nr. 9).

labours skilfully to discover the causes of misery, to find the means to combat it, to overcome it resolutely.'" (CiV, Nr. 30, which further cites the encyclical letter Populorum Progressio).

According to the encyclical letter, truth in the full sense is not something humans can simply produce autonomously. It always has the character of a gift that refers back to the giver, the God who is love and truth.[22] To put it more dramatically, the analysis of time and culture comes to a head in a "clear either-or" (CiV, Nr. 74). As can be seen in the field of "bioethics" in particular, we are forced through the enhancement of our technical opportunities to control nature and life to make a "choice": either we go the way of "moral responsibility" by choosing a "reason open to transcendence" or we go the irresponsible way in which we allow ourselves to be guided by a "reason closed within immanence" (CiV, Nr. 74). This reorientation can only take place by "purifying" reason (CiV, Nr 56). The necessary purifying force[23] can be found in faith which can reorient a constricted reason towards the "supernatural truth of charity" (CiV, Nr. 3). At this critical juncture, the argumentation becomes institutionally concrete. It is an "indirect" duty of the Roman Catholic Church "to contribute to the purification of reason and to the reawakening of . . . moral forces"; it is a "direct duty" for the "lay faithful" (DCE Nr. 29). An attentive Protestant observer, Joachim Track, already commented in 2008 after the Pope's lecture in Regensburg that, for the Pope, reason is essentially Catholic.[24]

What normative guidance should such a purified reason offer? The norms of a particular Roman Catholic understanding of natural law,[25] which takes up the early church's Logos speculations about the original

---

[22] "Reason, by itself, is capable of grasping the equality between men and of giving stability to their civic coexistence, but it cannot establish fraternity. This originates in a transcendent vocation from God the Father, who loved us first, teaching us through the Son what fraternal charity is." (CiV, Nr. 19).

[23] The metaphor of cleansing and sanitizing already plays a central role in Deus Caritas Est: "[i]f reason is to be exercised properly, it must undergo constant purification, since it can never be completely free of the danger of a certain ethical blindness caused by the dazzling effect of power and special interests." (DCE, Nr. 28 cf. also Nr. 10).

[24] Joachim Track, "Wie 'katholisch' ist die Vernunft? Anmerkungen zur Regensburger Vorlesung von Papst Benedikt XVI," in Konvent des Klosters Loccum, ed., Kirche in reformatorischer Verantwortung: Wahrnehmen – Leiten – Gestalten: Festschrift für Horst Hirschler (Göttingen: Vandenhoeck & Ruprecht, 2008), 231-249.

[25] "The Church's social teaching argues on the basis of reason and natural law, namely, on the basis of what is in accord with the nature of every human being" (DCE, Nr. 28, cf. also Nr. 31). For more on the broad and differentiated spectrum of teachings on natural law in Catholicism, cf. again Rudolf Uertz, Vom Gottesrecht zum Menschenrecht: Das katholische Staatsdenken in Deutschland von der Französischen Revolution bis zum II. Vatikanischen Konzil (1789-1965) (Paderborn: Schöningh, 2005).

divine reason [Urvernunft] pervading everything, etched also on the hearts of all people as the "universal moral law" (CiV, Nr. 59). The authorized interpreter of this teleological natural law is the Roman magisterium. Within the framework of this speculative synthesis of notions of order within the macro- and microcosm,[26] "nature" can be understood as expressing "a design of love and truth" (CiV, Nr. 48) and the doctrine of the Trinity is recommended as a "divine model" (CiV, Nr. 54) for relationships between human beings, indeed even for the "community of the human family" (CiV, Nr. 54). Joseph Ratzinger, who as a young theologian was once critical of the tradition of natural law because it could not account adequately for the temporality and historical situatedness of all guidance for action,[27] as Pope now reinvigorates the reasoning strategy of an ontological-metaphysical understanding of natural law. It is supposed to provide a unified bulwark to block the impetus towards differentiation and pluralization that paves the way to modern societies.

V.

Benedict XVI has reformulated classical themes of cultural criticism in his synopsis of metaphysics and the political consequences of his interpretation of the present. It would be interesting to discuss further which elements are shared across the different positions, belonging to the basic configuration even of the "new political theologies." Reading the encyclicals certainly causes one to remain aware of topics that need to be worked on when reflecting on the relationship between Christian orientations and political orders.

– Conceptions of history and diagnoses of crises are essential characteristics of the nature of political theologies. Indeed, even the "political path . . . of charity" (CiV, Nr. 7) is paved with an extensive critique of modernity. This includes a critique of natural science and technology. Despite attempts to differentiate itself clearly from Marxism, there is nevertheless a significant amount of agreement with the critique of "instrumental reason" in the Frankfurt School. The same can be said for his critique of market-based management models from the field of economics.

– The version of political theology advocated by the magisterium is critical of the principle of majority rule in political decision-making

---

[26] Ernst Topitsch, "Kosmos und Herrschaft: Ursprünge der 'politischen Theologie,'" in Wort und Wahrheit: Monatsschrift für Religion und Kultur 10/1 (1955), 19-30. He characterizes this idea as a "socio-cosmic universe" (19).

[27] Joseph Ratzinger, "Naturrecht, Evangelium und Ideologie in der katholischen Soziallehre: Katholische Erwägungen zum Thema," in Christlicher Glaube und Ideologie, ed. Klaus v. Bismarck and Walter Dirks, (Stuttgart: Kreuz-Verlag, 1964), 24-30.

processes. True reason illuminated by love and strengthened by hope does not need any procedural system of opinion-forming and decision-making. This already implies a critique of parliamentary democratic procedures. There are supposed to be areas that are never to be put to a vote, in which political decisions based on majority opinion are morally illegitimate. The Roman magisterium declares itself the last resort responsible for these areas that are withdrawn from the political process. Political theologies are associated with ecclesiologies. A comparison of these sometimes explicit, sometimes implicit ecclesiologies remains to be done.

– The elements of cultural critique are frequently packaged as a critique of liberalism. It is one of the striking convergences between "political theologies" of all stripes that they agree in their critique of "liberal" traditions. The role of so-called formal procedures and the positive legal system as well as reflection on the concrete political forms and constitutions of communal life play a subordinate role to basic ethical considerations. In contrast to procedures and pluralism, an ethical approach is posited by way of formulas about the common good. This ethical approach is based more on appellative claims than clear argumentation.

– Political theologies must elaborate an understanding of reason and rationality that can be communicated beyond theological circles and the church. The "enlightenment" about the Enlightenment has reinforced the need to take into account just how embedded in context all concepts of rationality are, how historically conditioned and dependent on dimensions of corporeality they are.[28] With his reference to the semantics of love and his understanding of reason, Benedict articulates a starting point from which one could initiate the process of overcoming a simple dualism such as "Reason versus Affect,"[29] but then he quickly spiritualizes precisely this correlation in a one-sided way through meta-

---

[28] For more on the difficulties of establishing claims to validity that transcend context despite the awareness of contingency and contradictions, cf. Jürgen Habermas, "Die Einheit der Vernunft in der Vielheit ihrer Stimmen," in idem, Nachmetaphysisches Denken (Frankfurt: Suhrkamp, 1988), 153-186. The metaphor-laden depiction is striking: "Communicative reason is certainly an endangered little boat in choppy waters—but it does not sink in the sea of contingencies, even though the swelling of the open sea is the only mode for it to 'come to terms with' contingencies" (185).

[29] The impetus for the theory construction of the young Hegel came precisely at this point: Cf. Jürgen Habermas, "Arbeit und Interaktion. Bemerkungen zu Hegels Jenenser Philosophie des Geistes (1967)," in idem, Technik und Wissenschaft als "Ideologie" 10th ed. (Frankfurt: Publ. 1979), 9-46. Jürgen Habermas saw in Hegel's reflections on the rational content of the Christian idea of love the prefiguration of the model for an unforced nature of the dialogical recognizing-oneself-in-the-other," which became the central idea for his own understanding of a communicative "Reason" based on the philosophy of language and theory of argumentation (17).

physical arguments. The ancient unhistorical Logos traditions and ontological natural law doctrines are unhelpful for addressing the problem of the situatedness of reason in a history which is always concrete. Acknowledging the historicality of reason and of our existence also in theology is a challenge sui generis,[30] considering that so-called "theological rationales" are often associated with a rapid withdrawal from the actual concrete historical situation, a dehistoricizing of validity claims, which then makes it possible to leap with apparent ease over the "ugly broad ditch" (Lessing) time and again.

– Modern cognitive contexts and cultures greet with skepticism any master plans ("world views") that reach into the metaphysical. Anyone who wishes to bring the unavoidable last questions into play must thus work hard to develop arguments that cannot be bypassed with moral pleas. On the path towards modernity, leeway for freedom was thus won precisely by scrutinizing sweeping validity claims and exposing them to the test of public discourse and debate. The more strongly concepts of reason appeal to strong notions of unity and teleological master plans, the greater the danger that "theoretical" differences and real conflicts will be too quickly hedged interpretively and pacified. An important touchstone for how much realism such schemes contain is certainly the manner in which they handle the irreducibly confrontational nature and meaninglessness of which human life is so full. Any theory of reconciliation is only as strong as its ability to apprehend differences indeed as differences.

– In the development of each theory of rationality, what is also at stake is the nature of institutions in which such a claim to a reasonable way of life can be concretely lived out: In which institutions is freedom possible and can a reasonable validity claim be made? A "political theology" which cannot indicate more concretely which institutional arrangements will allow us to increase our potential for rationality remains relatively blind and ineffectual. The form, the institutional

---

[30] Johann Baptist Metz begins with precisely this point with his insistence on a "Verzeitlichung von Ontologie und Metaphysik" or his concept of an "anamnetischen Vernunft" (cf. Metz, "Exkurs zu §8. Verzeitlichung von Ontologie und Metaphysik [1996]" in idem., Zum Begriff der neuen Politischen Theologie (Mainz: Matthias-Grünewald Verlag, 1997), 160-62; as well as idem, "Anamnetische Vernunft. Anmerkungen eines Theologen zur Krise der Geisteswissenschaften," in Zwischenbetrachtungen: Im Prozeß der Aufklärung, Jürgen Habermas zum 60. Geburtstag, ed. Axel Honneth et al (Frankfurt: Suhrkamp, 1989), 733-738. Jürgen Habermas tries to reduce the potential for confusion about historical contingency with basic assumptions from evolutionary theory and the philosophy of language. But the problem of historical situatedness cannot be completely avoided. This can be seen in his deeming a "self-critical politics of rememberance" as necessary to legitimate the political form of a constitutional democracy (cf. Habermas, "Vorpolitische Grundlagen des demokratischen Rechtsstaates?" in idem., Zwischen Naturalismus und Religion (Frankfurt: Suhrkamp, 2005), 106-118).

arrangement that has played a key role in the field of modern politics is representative democracy. The legitimation and limits of this form of communal life are still being fiercely contested even in the present. Are "values" necessary, and who is then responsible for the tradition and development of "values"?

In political theologies, the key term "political" often remains too vague. Politics has to do with human life together. Forms of communal life are subject to historical change. It makes a difference whether the benchmark (the "political") is an absolutist or theocratic state, the concept of a national bourgeois society, a liberal constitutional state, a "civil society," or an international "global community." The objectives of a political order, for which "political theologies" are formulated, and the actors towards which it is directed, need to be clearly identified.

– An original impulse for political theology can be seen in how political theologies are aligned with or differentiate themselves from Carl Schmitt. Schmitt's political theology was also contextual and driven by a specific political intention. He was not seeking to delegitimate something timeless, but was attacking specifically the Weimar parliamentary democracy. As the debate focused solely on Schmitt—both pros and cons—another view has been strongly suppressed: that of Hans Kelsen, whom fashionable theological circles quickly dismiss with the catchword "legal positivist." In 1929 Hans Kelsen wrote a short text: On the Essence and Value of Democracy[31] in which he focused on a topic that still presents a challenge for systematic reflection on political forms and their pre-political presuppositions.[32] Kelsen took the view that modern democracy can best be justified by forgoing claims to knowledge about absolute goodness and metaphysics. When such knowledge is claimed, then only the demand for obedience over against this knowledge can be made. The inner logic of democratic organization, however, lies precisely in making do with "relative truths attainable by human knowledge."[33] From this perspective, that which is often branded "relativism"[34] by strong concepts of reason is actually

---

[31] Hans Kelsen, *Vom Wesen und Wert der Demokratie*, 2nd ed. (Tübingen: Mohr, 1929).

[32] This was the main topic of discussion between Jürgen Habermas and Joseph Cardinal Ratzinger on 19 January 2004 in the Catholic Academy in Bavaria published in Zur Debatte: Themen der katholischen Theologie in Bayern 34/1 (2004). Available online in German at http://www.kath-akademie-bayern.de/-ausgabe/2004/1.html. At that time Ratzinger still expressed skepticism towards the tradition of natural law: "Natural law has remained—especially in the Catholic Church—the type of reasoning with which they . . . appeal to a common rationality and seek the foundations for an agreement about the ethical principles of the law in a secular, pluralistic society. But this instrument has become dull, unfortunately, and thus I do not wish to rely on it in this conversation" (Zur Debatte, 18).

[33] Kelsen, 100.

[34] Ibid., 101.

the lifeblood of democracy.[35] This view also leads to a critical stance towards theories of the common good, for the concept of common good can never be determined beforehand from some sort of superior position. Rather, it is the result of articulating interests and carrying out such conflicts. From this perspective, openly expressing the particularity of one's own interests is not ethically reprehensible, but an indispensable element of life in the search for truth and forms of a "good life."

---

[35] Further support for this argument can be found in Klaus Tanner, *Die fromme Verstaatlichung des Gewissens: Zur Auseinandersetzung um die Legitimität der Weimarer Reichsverfassung in Staatsrechtswissenschaft und Theologie der zwanziger Jahre* (Göttingen: Vandenhoek & Ruprecht, 1989).

Photo © Stefan Kresin. Used by permission.

Michael Welker

The Future Tasks of Political Theology: On Religion and Politics Beyond Habermas and Ratzinger

Herbert Vorgrimler collected numerous political-theological texts and statements of Karl Rahner, publishing them posthumously in 1986 as *Politische Dimensionen des Christentums: Ausgewählte Texte zu Fragen der Zeit* [Political Dimensions of Christianity: Selected Texts on Contemporary Questions].[1] He documents how Karl Rahner self-critically corrected his theological withdrawal into metaphysics and transcendental philosophy, as well as generalistic perspectives about "the human being," in order to make more space within his own thought for reflections on a political theology that is socioethically responsible.

Friendly but insistent admonitions by Rahner's students, especially Johann Baptist Metz, affected this development along with Rahner's own sense of "the situation," the spirit of the age, and his keen sense for humanistic values such as tolerance, fairness and justice. Due to his self-correction and the expansion of his thought, Rahner's voice continues to speak in a plethora of contextual, liberation, and feminist theologies, as well as other theologies that critique society, whether primarily reflecting theologically on memory, practical issues of justice, or eschatology. Through which forms and praxis would a Political Theology of the future be able to make good use of this wealth of isights and experience?

In searching for an answer to this question, we have sought in this book to engage in an important if limited discourse designated by the overarching theme "From Rahner to Ratzinger." Our goal has been not merely to provide an overview of a series of fascinating inner-Catholic dialogues. Rather, we have been seeking an ecumenical, international, and academic Political Theology of the future that is open to and active in civil society. What should such a Political Theology look like?

The following essay takes as its starting point a critical encounter between Jürgen Habermas and Josef Cardinal Ratzinger, a contrast of positions as provocative as it is instructive for the development of a Political Theology of the future.

The conversation between Habermas and Ratzinger took place January

---

[1] Herbert Vorgrimler, ed., *Karl Rahner, Politische Dimensionen des Christentums: Ausgewählte Texte zu Fragen der Zeit* (Kösel: München, 1986).

19, 2004 in Munich in the Catholic Academy of Bavaria and its subject was "The Pre-Political Moral Foundations of a Liberal State."[2] The organizers of the event talked about how "one could hardly imagine two more fascinating dialogue partners to reflect on the basic questions of human existence" (13 and 11). They saw in Ratzinger the "personification of the Catholic faith," and in Habermas "the personification of liberal, individual and secular thought" (12), and in both persons the "prototypes of a decisive dialogue in our day which will shape the future of our own world" (14).

I. Habermas on the "Democratic Process"

Despite these high expectations, the outcome and insights gained from this encounter—published in the form of two lectures—were rather modest. As he had done already in his famous acceptance speech for the peace prize of the German Booksellers in October 2001 in Frankfurt, Habermas offered an updated version of an *"Aufhebung* of religion" à la Kant and Hegel. Following an approach strongly reminiscent of Kant's *Religion within the Limits of Reason Alone,*[3] Habermas argues in this speech that secular society risks cutting itself off from "important resources for creating meaning" if it does not "retain a feeling for the expressive power of religious language."[4] In keeping with Kant's and Hegel's *Aufhebung* of religious content in both senses— *Aufhebung* as "sublation" but also as "maintenance"—Habermas advised the citizens of the liberal state to consider the religious source of the state's moral foundations so as to recover what he calls "the expressive level of one's own history of origins." He is particularly interested in "sin," "resurrection" and the "imago dei" as concepts whose power to provide moral and political orientation should not be lost.

Like Ratzinger, Habermas warns against a naturalistic-scientistic ideology which seeks to explain and describe everything scientifically, reducing personal and social human existence to nothing more than

---

[2] The dialogue was published by Academy director Florian Schuller in German as *Dialektik der Säkularisierung: Über Vernunft und Religion* (Herder: Freiburg, 2005). The English translation was published as *The Dialectics of Secularization: On Reason and Religion* (San Francisco: Ignatius Press, 2007). Page numbers (in parentheses) refer to the original German edition. Quotes were translated by the translator of this article. Some of the reflections that follow in this article can also be found within the context of a more detailed analysis and critique in "Habermas und Ratzinger zur Zukunft der Religion," *Evangelische Theologie* 68 (2008), 310-324 and in English as "Habermas and Ratzinger on the Future of Religion," *Scottish Journal of Theology* 63/4 (2010), 456-473.

[3] Immanuel Kant, *Die Metaphysik der Sitten*, vol. 8, *Werke*, ed. Wilhelm Weischedel (Frankfurt: Suhrkamp, 1956).

[4] www.glasnost.de/docs01/011014habermas.html. The following citations come from this speech and were translated by the translator of this article.

natural processes. He calls for such an ideologically "bad philosophy" to be enlightened through philosophical and scientific approaches as well as religious ones. Secularization must be prevented from being "derailed." According to Habermas, this should not lead to the conviction, however, that the liberal secularized state is indeed "dependent on traditions specific to one particular worldview, locality or religion or, at any rate, on collectively-binding ethical traditions" (16).[5]

This recognition this does not presume the existence of a state authority that is to be domesticated by religious or other means. Rather, in the current social reality of the "democratic process" we must pay attention to the "inclusive and discursive process of opinion formation and decision-making" by citizens. This process requires only "weak presuppositions about the normative content of the communicative nature of socio-cultural forms of life" (19). According to Habermas, these weak presuppositions are fulfilled when the following is true about the results of communication about the basic guidelines for life styles: it is expected and demanded that they be rationally acceptable—even to the point that they could constitute constitutional principles. On this basis the legal regulation of state authority, continuously underwritten by loyalty, can occur. A stable power arrangement is thereby in place that does not require any higher "maintaining power" of a religious or other nature.

Habermas sees in modern secular societies a two-class system made up of "citizens of the state who understand themselves as authors of the law," on the one hand, and "citizens of society who are addressees of the law" (22), on the other. The democratic process Habermas has in mind is apparently designed to help the "citizens of society concerned with their own well-being" see themselves more and more as "citizens of the state" and correspondingly behave in a way that is well informed about law and politics and that seeks influence in this sphere. These citizens, conscious of their power as authors of the law, are to strengthen continually the "uniting bond of the democratic process." By competing for the best interpretation of controversial constitutional principles, they are to keep this process alive.

Habermas affirms what he calls a self-critical "politics of memory" and a "constitutional patriotism" which value and constantly reappraise constitutional principles discursively in the contemporary context. Just as Immanuel Kant saw the coming of the kingdom of God on earth in faithful obedience to the categorical imperative, so Jürgen Habermas sees the emergence of an ever-stronger solidarity of "citizens of the state" through a "democratic process" supported by a self-critical politics of memory, constitutional patriotism, the subjection of state power to legal procedures, and rational standards to enforce this con-

---

[5] Cf. the critical discussion in Judith Butler et al, *The Power of Religion in the Public Sphere* (New York: Columbia University Press, 2011).

trol. These "citizens of the state," as self-confident authors of the law, influence these "principles of justice" so that they increasingly reflect the "dense network of ethical orientations in a culture" (25). Yet Habermas remains aware of how profoundly illusory this vision may be and reflects on this danger in a section entitled: "When the social bond breaks . . ." (26).

Above all it is the power of the market and especially the "politically uncontrollable dynamics of the global economy and society" (26) which cause Habermas to fear a "derailment of modernization" and erosion of bourgeois solidarity. In my opinion Habermas described the dangers to the "democratic process," especially from electronic mass media, much more forcefully and more realistically back in 1990 in the lengthy preface to the new edition of his book *The Structural Transformation of the Public Sphere*[6] and again in 1992 in *Between Facts and Norms*[7]. He summed up the situation somewhat skeptically in *Between Facts and Norms*:

"The sociology of mass communications certainly conveys a skeptical image of the public sphere of Western democracies dominated by mass media (as reduced to a mere power struggle) ... While many groupings in civil society are indeed sensitive to problems, when they express their concerns, their signals and impulses are generally too weak to catalyze short-term learning processes or redirect political decision-making processes."[8]

In my opinion, in this earlier work Habermas adopts a more down-to-earth and realistic view of the situation, conceding that the associations in civil society (including the "democratic process") are not "the most conspicuous elements of a public sphere dominated by the mass media and major agencies, observed and analyzed by marketing and public opinion research groups, and steeped in public relations, propaganda, and advertising by political parties and organizations."[9]

In his conversation with Ratzinger, Habermas recommends that all citizens of "postsecular society" as well as state constitutional authorities "deal carefully with the cultural wellsprings which feed into the

---

[6] *The Structural Transformation of the Public Sphere: An Inquiry into a Category of Bourgeois Society* (Cambridge, MA: MIT Press, 1991). German original: *Strukturwandel der Öffentlichkeit: Untersuchungen zu einer Kategorie der bürgerlichen Gesellschaft* (Frankfurt: Suhrkamp, 1990).

[7] *Between Facts and Norms: Contributions to a Discourse Theory of Law and Democracy* (Cambridge, UK: Polity Press, 1996). German original: *Faktizität und Geltung: Beiträge zur Diskurstheorie des Rechts und des demokratischen Rechtsstaats* (Frankfurt: Suhrkamp, 1992);

[8] Ibid., 451. Cf. my critique of the already shaky defense against a "colonization of one's political environment" in M. Welker, *Kirche im Pluralismus*, 2nd ed. (Gütersloh: Kaiser, 2000), Chapt. 1.

[9] Ibid., 444.

consciousness of norms and the solidarity of all citizens" (32f). Philo-sophically-articulated and -cultivated forms of religiosity and secular thinking should learn from one another, serving to protect and strengthen social solidarity. This solidarity should be nourished through the democratic process to resist the power of the market and seemingly value-neutral governments. "For the time being," Habermas argues, we should expect "the continued existence of religious com-munities." They should be so integrated into the processes of civil so-ciety that they are instrumental to them. Those citizens of the state who are philosophically, morally, legally and religiously informed should therefore "participate in the effort to translate relevant contributions from a religious mode of expression into a language accessible to the public." (36)

The concept of the communicative processes of civil society which Habermas shares in this historic conversation offers two significant and thought-provoking insights for Political Theology. Habermas insists on a permanent public discourse whose goal is an ongoing process of so-cietal stabilization and change, although he is guided by the standards of the constitution of a state that presents itself as a constitutional and social welfare state. Furthermore, Habermas sees that mere ideas about social change and mere moral appeals are insufficient. Visions of emancipation and liberation as well as moral commitments must be converted into legislation and legal action.

While these impulses should be taken to heart, I believe this concept reflects philosophical wishful thinking. It is hardly a suitable model for a serious Political Theology. For while Habermas exhibits a good sense of which central theological subjects have untapped potential to provide political-moral orientation, he fails to appreciate adequately the religious power in ecclesial and academic institutions and the com-municative processes of civil society. The power of church and academy, educational systems and families, media and art to shape reli-gion must all be taken into account. Simply trusting in self-selective elites who have gained public prominence as model citizens of the state and authors of the law leads to an ideal conception of civil society that obscures real power relations.

II. Ratzinger and Trust in Natural Law

While Joseph Cardinal Ratzinger grasps the nature of the problem in a significantly more defensive way than Habermas, his approach also re-flects a global breadth that is missing in Habermas's perspective as a philosopher concentrated on Germany and Western democracies. Ratzinger wishes to pose the question of what he calls the "ethical con-trols on power" (40). From the outset he perceives "legally accountable

forms of restraining and organizing power" (40) as an intercultural
problem. For this reason, the important quest for the ethical foundations which "guide the coexistence (of cultures) in the right direction"
cannot be entrusted solely to discourse groups within society.

In addition to this global perspective, Ratzinger expresses ethical skepticism. "In the process of cultural encounter and mutual penetration,"
the traditional, fundamental "ethical certainties have largely disin-
tegrated" and the question of "what is the good, and why one must do
it, even to one's own detriment" remains "largely" unanswered (40).
The abandonment of tradition, a lack of moral orientation and an un-
willingness to make sacrifices all pose grave problems. Like Habermas, he concentrates on the link between moral and legal processes of
development. He formulates it succinctly: "Not the law of the strong
but the strength of the law must rule." Politics is therefore accorded the
task of placing "power under the criterion of the law," making "jointly-
shared freedom" possible (42).

At this juncture Ratzinger's and Habermas's approaches come closer
together even as they maintain a careful distance. According to
Ratzinger, the law must be the "vehicle of justice" and "expression of
the common interest shared by all." This militates in favor of democracy "as the most appropriate form of political order" (42 and 43). At
the same time, "the tools of democratic decision-making" solve the
problems associated with democracy—at least "for now" (42f). The
fact that majorities and democratically-elected delegations can be cor-
rupted begs the question whether there are injustices that can never be
made right and whether there are inalienable laws no majority is able to
abrogate (cf. 43).

Ratzinger sees in modern declarations of rights an attempt to secure the
foundations of the law. As an indication of the very diverse levels of
acceptance these human rights have been accorded in various cultures
in the world, he writes:

the contemporary mindset is certainly satisfied with the inherent obviousness of
these values. But even such self-limitation in asking the question has a certain
philosophical character. There are inherent values which result from the nature of
being human and therefore are inalienable for all those who possess this nature
(43f).

Ratzinger's answers to the burning question of where to find "independent values that follow from the nature of being human" sound
vague and uncertain. Within the Catholic Church "natural law" has remained "the model for argumentation which the church uses in discussions with secular society and other faith communities to appeal to
common reason and in the search for a foundation of agreement on the
ethical principles of the law in a secular, pluralistic society" (50). He
observes with some regret, however, that "this tool has lost its ef-

fectiveness unfortunately" (50). He calls for the retrieval of those values and norms "inherent to human existence"[10] which cannot be considered mere inventions. He calls on philosophy and a Christian theology of creation to join in the search for sustainable foundations for natural law inherent to human existence, and he challenges the other major religious traditions of the world to take part in this project. He envisions a "polyphonous correlation" in which the various major religions would achieve constructive and peaceful relationships with secular rationality and in this way engage in mutual dialogue. In this event the fundamentals of natural law would be recognizable in a new way so that the "essential values and norms which are known or sensed by all people could attain a new luminosity" (58).

It is striking that Ratzinger's universal concept is even more heavily reliant on philosophical wishful thinking than that of Habermas. Aside from the metaphysical presupposition of a theologically-viable natural law—which is problematic and calls for critical discussion—this concept is also theologically empty. If one does not count his grim assumptions about widespread relativism and moral decline as a social-analytical contribution, then one must realistically ascertain that a serious diagnosis is also largely absent. He barely articulates the substantial cultural, societal, and political differences associated with the major religions. Speculative wishful thinking about natural law suggests a power to connect and integrate which does not remotely correspond to the real circumstances. While global perspectives are intended, they are not realistically developed in even a rudimentary way.

III. What must a Political Theology of the future accomplish?

Aside from specific contextual analyses for crisis and conflict situations, a Political Theology of the future must develop the ability to perceive matters theologically and pneumatologically, and it must combine this perception with a desire to engage in social analysis. In developing an empirical interest in pneumatological theology and social analysis, the brilliant dissertation of the young Dietrich Bonhoeffer *Sanctorum Communio* can provide a model for the first stage of analysis. It develops a high level of social-theoretical awareness.[11]

Bonhoeffer sees that our perception and discourse about "the human,"

---

[10] For more on this, see the critical examination by Klaus Tanner in this volume.

[11] Dietrich Bonhoeffer, *Sanctorum Communio: Eine dogmatische Untersuchung zur Soziologie der Kirche*, DBW Vol. I (Kaiser: München 1986). English edition: *Sanctorum Communio: A Theological Study of the Sociology of the Church*, vol. 1, *Works* (Fortress Press: Minneapolis, MN, 2009). Cf. Michael Welker, *Theologische Profile: Schleiermacher—Barth—Bonhoeffer—Moltmann* (Frankfurt: Edition Chrismon, 2009).

the person and the individual, as well as our discourse about community, society, and the public are rife with presuppositions. The perception of the individual human being and social conditions interact with visions of "humanity" and all the visible and hidden value systems with which we associate them. Yet it is not only our perceptions of the human being and humanity that are mutually shaping one another, but also the ways we think about I-You relationships and the ethos of personal encounters. How we understand both normal and ideal social relationships interacts with our concepts of the individual human being and humanity as a whole. Beyond this we must distinguish between fixed institutionalized relationships and fluid social ones. In this case, various interconnections come into play in our concepts of normality and development related to when we speak of the individual, humanity, or intimate relationships. Ultimately, our images and concepts of God are normatively interconnected within this complex social network in manifold ways.

Bonhoeffer considers several basic social constellations,[12] in which each of the following elements is considered in terms of their multifaceted interdependencies:

- the self-relation of the human being,
- the interpersonal I-You relationship,
- relationships to complex fixed and fluid forms of sociality,
- and the relationship to God.

The understanding of the person, the concept of God, the elementary one-on-one personal relationship and complex social relations—fixed and fluid—all exist in manifold non-arbitrary correlations to one another. Instead of an abstract relationship between God's relationship to me, we need to grasp the correlations between God's relationship to my fellow human beings and the relationship between me, my fellow human beings and to the broader social environment. Moreover we need to grasp finally the human reference to God. Yet even these correlations do not tell the whole story.

Bonhoeffer first distinguishes between four major non-theological constellations which organize this complex pattern of correlations conceptually. He distinguishes between four constellations from history and intellectual history (Aristotle, the Stoics, Epicurus, and European philosophers of modernity, especially Descartes and Kant) in which the interdependencies between the concept of God, the concept of the person, the "I-You" relationship, and the concept of community can be understood differently: This prompts him to consider various schemata

---

[12] Cf. *Sanctorum Communio*, 19.

of complex social relationships including their religious components,[13] guided by studies of the history of philosophy. Only after this does he develop specifically theological figures of human sociality under the headings "the humankind of Adam" and "the humankind of Christ."[14]

1) A Political Theology of the future must practice and help practice such social-theoretical awareness as the first step of political-theoretical reasoning. It must be relentlessly clear that purely dialogistic models (I and the Other) are useless in general for grasping complex social relations. In the same way it is inadequate to apply family models to conceive of political or even global relations.[15] There is only limited potential to intellectual approaches obsessed with "the individual and society," "subject and society" and abstract relationships such as "God and the human being" and "God and the world," to name just the most primitive examples. Guided by a broader social-theoretical awareness, a Political Theology of the future must attempt to develop socioanalytical honesty.

One's close circle of friends and interest groups, the local church parish, the academic community, and the public spheres of the regional and international media represent only small cross-sections of the societies in which we live. A Political Theology which seeks to understand social and political processes of development theologically and wishes to initiate and assist in guiding these processes must be able to comprehend and interpret individual societal contexts including the particular institutional—as well as social and moral—power dynamics which surround them. It must make clear that efforts for "neutral observation" are also guided by naïve interests or even apparent or latent ideologies. And it must attempt to uncover and differentiate between these power interests and incorporate them within a theological interpretative framework.

2) When engaging in socioanalytical studies, we cannot simply apply the organizational forms of the pluralistic societies in which Europeans and North Americans live today to all other societies on earth in past and present.[16] Pluralistic societies require a multi-systemic approach which first calls for a self-critical positioning of Political Theology in the church, in the academy, and in civil society.[17] Almost thirty years ago David Tracy provided the impetus for such subtle observations.[18]

---

[13] Cf. ibid., 20ff.

[14] Ibid., 69; Cf. 36, 69ff, 74ff.

[15] See the essay by Klaus Tanner on Benedict XVI in this volume.

[16] Jürgen Moltmann has made this argument repeatedly and emphatically. See also his essay in this volume.

[17] See the instructive text by Chantal Mouffee, *Über das Politische: Wider die kosmopolitische Illusion*, (Frankfurt: Suhrkamp, 2007).

[18] David Tracy, *The Analogical Imagination: Christian Theology and the Culture*

Unfortunately, he did not capture the full spectrum of societal systems with "the church," "the academy" and "civil society" and he failed to engage in a serious further development of this analytical approach. The analysis of the pluralistic situation became too diffuse in *Plurality and Ambiguity*. The complex interplay and conflicts between systemic organizations and social institutions and the associations of a civil society have not been adequately appreciated in most approaches to a pluralistic Political Theology.[19]

Most approaches to Political Theology are oriented towards local parishes and civil societies, if they develop any true awareness of contexts at all. They generally hope to inspire further analysis in the areas of the media, academy, church politics, and politics in general. The interdependencies of politics and law, politics and the economy, and politics and the power of the media are grasped only vaguely at best. For this reason many contributions to Political Theology remain stuck in the medium of describing problems and making moral appeals and laments.

But a lack of social-theoretical awareness and a want of socioanalytical potential are closely related to problems finding topical theological orientation.

3) A Political Theology of the future must develop a social-theoretical awareness and socioanalytical diagnostics in the context of its theological-pneumatological observations. A genuinely pneumatological orientation requires that every discourse about "the human being" and "humanity" be continually differentiated. The Holy Spirit aims at a differentiated unity of humanity in which differences that are unjust and detrimental to life are overcome, while creative differences are retained and cultivated. God's Spirit is poured out on men and women, young and old, the privileged and the disadvantaged, yes, even the oppressed, as expressed in the biblical promises.[20] Sexist, ageist and social conflicts—and the potential for conflict—thus come into view. Ethnic, linguistic, and cultural differences are not simply eliminated through the activity of the Spirit, but rather they are integrated into complex communicative interactions

In this way, the power of the Spirit not only stabilizes the differentiated contexts of shared human life. The biblical traditions also provide numerous images in which both stability and dynamics are connected in the power of the Spirit. Speaking about the "Body of Christ" with its various gifts and charismas definitely has the potential to guide social

---

of Pluralism (Crossroad: New York, 1981), esp. 3ff.

[19] For more, see Michael Welker, *Kirche im Pluralismus* 2nd ed. (Gütersloh: Gütersloher Verlagshaus, 2000).

[20] See Joel 3 and Acts 2; see M. Welker, *Gottes Geist: Theologie des Heiligen Geistes,* 4th ed. (Neukirchener, Neukirchen-Vluyn, 2010). Available in English as *God the Spirit* (Augsburg Fortress Press: Minneapolis, 2004).

communicative processes. It stands in tension with stratified, mono-hierarchical, patriarchal structures in many societies and churches and thus also develops highly topical political dynamics. Yet a pneumatological orientation does not simply offer idealized images of harmony and successful interdependence. There remain manifold tensions between the "Spirit of justice, of truth and of love" and real circumstances in which people are marginalized, repressed, and disenfranchised in glaringly awful and brutal ways but also in more latent forms.[21] The Spirit compels us then to prophetic and diaconal resistance in societal, social, and cultural conflict situations.

A Political Theology must name such specific conflict situations and grasp them with social-theoretical awareness and socioanalytical honesty. It will run up against numerous processes that are negative and detrimental to life which stabilize dishonesty and injustice, including opposition and violence.[22] This pneumatological orientation brings into focus nothing less than the intense confrontation between the kingdom of God and the Spirit of God, on the one hand, and the human being who has been seized by the power of sin, on the other.[23] Again and again Political Theology must perceive the powerlessness and the limits of moral and legal power.

As a doctoral student of Metz and Rahner and inspired by Ernst Bloch, Francis Fiorenza pursued the question of why fascism was more successful than communism in Germany in the 1920s.[24] One answer was that fascism was closer to bourgeois society with its moral values and ideologies. Political Theology, according to Fiorenza, should analyze and appreciate the value system and power structures of modern bourgeois society in all its ambivalences. Such concrete examinations of politics with its symbols and power are indispensable for a Political Theology. They cannot cease even when positive political resonance, successful legislation, legal action or even perfect religious and moral organization have been achieved.

A Political Theology of the future will not be able to avoid a permanent conflict which critiques society, culture, religions and ideologies—even in the face of seemingly optimized and successful

---

[21] See especially the essay by Elisabeth Schüssler Fiorenza in this volume.

[22] For a contemporary consideration of this problem, cf. Jane Mayer, *The Dark Side: The Inside Story of How the War on Terror Turned into a War on American Ideals* (New York: Doubleday, 2008), and also the essay by Francis Schüssler Fiorenza in this volume.

[23] Cf. Sigrid Brandt, ed., *Sünde: Ein unverständlich gewordenes Thema* (Neukirchener, Neukirchen-Vluyn 1997).

[24] For more, see Francis Fiorenza, "Politische Theologie und liberale Gerechtigkeits-Konzeptionen," in Edward Schillebeeckx, ed., *Mystik und Politik: Theologie im Ringen um Geschichte und Gesellschaft*, Festschrift für Johann Baptist Metz (Grünewald: Mainz, 1988), 105ff.

political and religious achievements. According to insights from both New and Old Testaments, even the good Law is still subject to the power of sin. The powerlessness of the law due to the forces indicated biblically with the code word "sin" is opposed to the creative power of the divine Spirit. The Spirit releases prophetic, diaconal, liturgical and spiritual powers that transform, renew and elevate not just individual people and interpersonal relationships, but also social, societal, ecclesial, and political forms of life.

A Political Theology of the future will be a pneumatologically-oriented theology which makes honest use of social analysis and develops a critical awareness through social theory. It will make use of these orienting frameworks and impulses in concrete contextual experiences of oppression and suffering as well as in the flourishing of life, and in concrete prophetic and practical partisanship.

CPSIA information can be obtained at www.ICGtesting.com
Printed in the USA
LVOW08s0952301013

359079LV00002B/86/P